Too Pretty to be Good

A memoir

TOO Pretty TO BE GOOD

By Lindsay Byron

So you mustn't be frightened, dear Mr. Kappus, if a sadness rises in front of you, larger than any you have ever seen; if an anxiety, like light and cloud-shadows, moves over your hands and over everything you do. You must realize that something is happening to you, that life has not forgotten you, that it holds you in its hand and will not let you fall. Why do you want to shut out of your life any uneasiness, any misery, any depression, since after all you don't know what work these conditions are doing inside you? Why do you want to persecute yourself with the question of where all this is coming from and where it is going? Since you know, after all, that you are in the midst of transitions and you wished for nothing so much as to change. If there is anything unhealthy in your reactions, just bear in mind that sickness is the means by which an organism frees itself from what is alien; so one must simply help it to be sick, to have its whole sickness and to break out with it, since that is the way it gets better. In you, dear Mr. Kappus, so much is happening now; you must be patient like someone who is sick, and confident like someone who is recovering; for perhaps you are both.

Rainer Maria Rilke, *Letters to a Young Poet*

These signs lined the way from the dressing room to the stage at the classiest joint I ever worked.

A Great Many Things

The truth comes out.

The women who raised me are old and dying, and no secret ever loved a grave.

Where I come from, the great aunts are aplenty, beauty queens from another century. As a girl, I studied them: long nails red like their lips, sweaters stretched over ample busts, smiles that are closed doors, no complaints and no entry. *There are a great many things about these women that we do not know*, Mama always told me, growing up.

When I was young, I drew self-portraits by the moonlight of my bedroom window, scribbling in crayon a woman on a pedestal with a painted face and a crooked smile, all curves and mystery. *Me When I Grow Up*, I would title these pieces, a prophecy scrawled in Blue Cyan. When my mother found my drawings, she worried that I had become enamored with whores. Little did she know, it was her, us, our foremothers I was drawing.

A troubled youth, they'll say, daddy issues—these are the citations people will give when explaining why a girl turns into a woman like me. I am guilty of all of these and more. Yet stronger than these streams leading ever toward my fate, there is one reason that never makes the list: a portrait of a goddess, drawn by a child in the dark.

Every Christmas, my family gathers at Granny Audrey's house. My generation is the first to move away from Danville, a dead mill town on the north side of the Virginia-North Carolina line. If you rearrange the letters in Danville, it spells Evilland. In this, the final capital of the Confederacy, tobacco once was king, but now Oxycontin takes the throne. The jobs all moved to Mexico, the storefronts closed, and the young folks are on exodus. Growing up, the hottest things poppin' were weed circles in abandoned gas stations. Where I come from, we make love under the bridge just beyond the city line, a place called Twin Arches, the gravel in your back.

The holidays of my childhood were shadowed by my mama's extravagant depression. Sighing heavily in a corner, Mama and her sorrow begged witness while I unwrapped Barbies bought on credit and tried to hide my glee.

Mama lost her father when she was a young woman, right around Christmas time. His heart sputtered one good time, and then he was gone. His death wasn't even the first time he left her—just the last. With his final departure, Mama was thrust right back onto those front stairs, age of seven, wishing her daddy would walk back into their home. He would not.

I remember watching her drag shadows across each Christmas, thinking—*what a drama queen*. Why did she have to turn her misery into theater? The man had been dead in her life longer than he'd been living. I never met him. He meant little more to me than a photo in a frame and my mother's annual depression.

We're the kind of women who can't keep men, and no holiday in the world can erase that.

The women that came before me grew up in a sharecropper's cabin, no more than twenty miles from the respectable neighborhood where we now gather. Despite the fine suburban homes they've purchased since, none of them really ever left that shack, the dirt floor of their youths setting up residence as the ground floor of their hearts. Yet from that dirt, among tobacco fields and cotton, a crop of beautiful women bloomed, one-by-one. And one-by-one, they learned the power of a well-timed wink, an artfully-posed body, a smile that invites men to brag about themselves. *Always let a man talk,* Great Aunt Catherine told me, *and he'll give you anything.* In her ears hung diamonds that attested to this truth.

As we pass Christmas gifts around Granny Audrey's parlor, Great Aunt Ava enters. She hasn't been out in a while, recently released from the nursing home after another fall. *She's losing it,* the family whispers; *she's gotten so old.*

"Ava might've been the prettiest among 'em," Mama tells me in a whisper.

As Ava makes slow rounds, handing out hugs and hellos, her eyes alight on me. Her face is lined but painted nonetheless, mascara carefully applied, coral lipstick coordinated with coral earrings. Real women never die. She takes my chin in her hand and gazes upon my face. "True beauty," she marvels. At thirty-five, I feel ancient, an old hoe, but to her, I am a child, a lifetime ahead of me.

"Your granny has told me about your...job," she whispers, and darts her eyes around the room. She's not talking about my postdoc at Tech, not referring to the respectable career I have abandoned.

"Tell me," she whispers, leaning closer—"do they really call you Lux?"

What does she know about me? What is safe for me to say? Does she know I've built my life slinging lap dances in the dark? Does she know I became a doctor and then threw it all away?

Does she know I made a name for this family, the only one out of this long line of women to end up with a PhD; does she know I abandoned that? Couldn't hack it; back to stripping: this is who I am. A secret. Hidden selves locked in drawers: which ones do we open? Ava is in her eighties now and has worn a quiet smile for nearly a century. What parts of me can she understand?

"What do you know about me, exactly?"

"Honey," she says, "I know *everything*."

There are a great many things about these women that we do not know.

We have imaginations, however. And we have whispers. And in the space where imaginations meet whispers, legends are born.

The women in my family are ladies. The women in my family have secrets. The women in my family cloak that whirling dervish we call a heart and present a placid public face on shopping day, strolling through Winn Dixie humming a careless tune—Patsy Cline's "Crazy"—practiced nonchalance that announces to all passersby, *I'm just perfectly fine!* Throw a pretty face like a shroud over these sticky insides: this is woman's work.

In hushed tones in back bedrooms over dozens of years of Christmas suppers, we girls of the younger generation have stitched together the parts of our lineage that have been hidden, the puzzle pieces only alluded to when somebody got mad and mentioned the abortion, or the uncle who touched too much. We add our knowledge, subtract our family's predilection for exaggeration, and somewhere, between imaginations and whispers, we author legends.

Hidden pregnancies, girdles worn until the seventh month. High school weddings and homemade dresses. Men who tore doors off hinges. Men who rolled bodily down the driveway, blacked out on drink. Audrey, this is your neighbor calling, come collect your husband from the front yard. If Aunt Catherine was so lovely, why did she wear those big sunglasses? Oh. Her husband.

There is no truth that beauty cannot hide.

"Yes," I tell her, "they do call me Lux."

"Your husband don't mind you dancing for them men?" Ava asks. "Between you and me, honey—I've always been popular with them men."

"Ava's got—quite the past," Mama has remarked, upon occasion.

Merely a school girl, picked up at the bus stop on Tuesdays by a man in a Cadillac; she was only thirteen then. "Why didn't anyone stop this grown man from raping that child?" I demanded when I first heard the tale. In response Mama told me, well—he *was* handsome. Had him one of them Clark Gable moustaches.

Ava takes my hands into hers. This may be the last time I see her. This generation buries a sister every year now, leaving behind a collection of black and white photographs, costume jewelry, mythology, and mystery.

"I really was quite a bright woman," she says. "I could've been a lot of things."

At my knee, there is a tugging. I look down to find my tow-headed boy pulling on my pantleg, bright blue eyes looking up at me, in his hand a drawing he's made for his mama. He points to a painting on the wall. In it, a sailboat is tossed by a storm. In the corner of the canvas, in deft strokes I know so well, reads the name *David Burton*. "*My* daddy painted that," I tell my son, taking him by the hand. Of everyone who has ever loved me in this life, this boy whose hand I hold, and that dead man on the wall—these two have loved me the most.

My husband enters the room, his square jaw softening as he looks upon our son, as he finds his center in the soap opera that is home for the holidays. Behind him, a bevy of aunts gather. He's one of the few men here. *Would you like some banana pudding,* they ask; *would you like some sweet tea?* "Be nice to them," I warned him on the drive up. "No sarcastic jokes like last year."

"Lord Jesus," Ava says as her eyes wander from my son to my husband. "You just have it all. That's what you get when you're so pretty."

Me, pretty?

At one time, certainly that was true.

I approach the mirror in the hallway. These lines on my forehead, an atrocity of betrayal. And damned if my face isn't falling into a mask of my mother. I put my fingers at my temples and pull the skin back. *There.*

"Don't," Mama says, appearing by my side. As I release my temples, in the mirror I see just how right my fears have become: she and I, this mother and me—we are twins.

"Mama," I ask her, "why didn't Granny Potter stop that Cadillac man from sleeping with Great Aunt Ava?" I had known my great grandmother only briefly. I cannot well recall her. She had one rubber breast and a hardscrabble life and a lot on her mind.

"Granny couldn't be at all places at all times," Mama explains. Great Granny had nine children, plus the town doctor to assist on her few precious moments of free time. She hadn't an extra moment to spare, but when she did, she'd sometimes take an evening away, citing another birth in town. "Although—I never did see enough babies to account for all those nights she'd spent helping that doctor birth them," Mama laughs. "Everybody's got a secret life, little girl. Maybe even your great granny. Maybe even your own mama."

As I look upon my family gathered in this parlor, this same room where my mother was married for the first time at seventeen and my aunt at fifteen...the same coffee table my grandpa busted his nose on, toppling over drunk to meet Mama's first husband, Steve...the same door Steve tore through after Mama left him for my daddy, hollering into the family home that Linda sucks dick...this parlor, a stage upon which my family both enacts their dramas as well as relives them, is full again with conversation. Here stand my people, here they have stood for generations, concocting narratives to justify crimes, to polish dullness, to turn our awfulness into heroism, our horror into romance. Who among us now has my name on their lips? And if so, what name do they speak?

I'm worried they'll find out the full extent of me. I don't just dance on a stage, Aunt Ava. I am no Gypsy Rose Lee. Look at me. I'm an aged hoe. I had other options—good, respectable options—and yet this is what I chose. I know that not every stone can be shined into a gem, know that there are parts of me that can't be spun into poetry, know that there are pieces of me that are just flat-out bad, no romanticizing them away.

Ghosts of real events haunt this parlor like an angry ancestor, scratching holes into the stories we tell to look good, the twists we inject into the plots of our lives to retain some sense of decency. It's all speculation, legend, romance mixed up with the facts. That's the thing about secrets: they erect around themselves their own kind of truth.

"Everybody's got a secret life," Mama said.

Maybe—even me.

PART ONE

CHAPTER ONE
WILD THING

My daddy was an artist. That's the first thing I tell people about him. He made his money on his back, fixing machines weighing greater than four elephants, his skin stained eternally with grease—but in his free time, which was seldom, he took up a paintbrush, dainty.

"Some people ain't got no culture," Daddy told me, from time to time. "Not everybody can appreciate art."

On display throughout our home, Daddy's paintings proved that while we may not have the right manners or the right kinfolk, we damn sure had culture. Among masterpieces of landscapes and woodland creatures, Daddy hung calligraphic versions of my name all over his workroom walls—under his hand, *Lindsay* more elegant than anything I could ever write.

I, too, tried my hand at art. As always, beautiful women were my subject. For weeks, I studied my daddy's methods, the way he created darkness, captured light, made a few lines on a page come alive with a touch of shading and a smattering of white. I applied these methods myself, using gradients of black and grey to create a portrait of a woman's face, her mouth agape in a scream.

"It's the shadows on things that make them beautiful," Daddy remarked, nodding as he gazed upon my work.

I've made my life a poem about that.

He was like Elvis, my daddy—he had to die young to reach his potential.

I tried to kill myself when I was thirteen after Daddy caught me with a dick in my mouth.

But before that, me and him watched storms.

Watching storms together—that was a thing we did. Drawn to the black clouds and the flashes in between, we sat on the front porch, fat drops splashing against our legs, halfway wishing the thunder would transform into a hurricane. Inside, Mama migrated to the center of the home, crouched in a bathtub, afraid.

"You see that cloud out yonder, that real ugly one?" Daddy said. "I'm gonna paint that sumbitch."

Storms informed Daddy's art.

Before us, in the front yard, the velvety leaves of the magnolia whipped in the wind. Suddenly, a crack issued from the great tree, and with a crash the magnolia dropped a branch, scattering leaves into the yard. Daddy hopped to his feet and ran to the wreckage. I joined him at his side.

"Well, I'll be goddamned," he said. "There's a baby squirrel in there."

In the pounding rain, half-hidden beneath the leaves, a tiny creature padded the ground with its paws. Around it, its mother scampered, panicked.

When the storm died down, Daddy and I went out to check on the baby, and found it still searching, eyes sealed shut and tail as thin as a cat's. "He's too big for his mama to carry him back to the nest," Daddy remarked, judging the size of the baby in his hand, searching the tree for the mother who'd given up.

"Lord Jesus," Mama sighed when Daddy brought the squirrel into our home.

While Daddy left to purchase kitten formula and a tiny bottle with which to feed our new pet, I cradled the infant on my chest. If I held him long enough, I pondered, perhaps the first time he opened his eyes, he would see me. I wanted that—wanted this angel to open his eyes and see the whole world in me. By the time Daddy returned home, I'd decided on a name.

"I've named him Gabriel," I announced.

"That ain't no name for a squirrel," Daddy said, Marlboro balanced on his bottom lip. He took one hammer-flattened finger and scratched the baby beneath his soft chin.

"His name is Fred."

I can't blame the suicide attempt, or the circus of self-destructive behaviors that followed, solely on Daddy's discovery of me sucking dick. Fact is, I've been authoring my own nightmares since I can remember.

Most parents worry about finding their children playing doctor, or maybe using drugs. In my time, I've been convicted on both counts. But perhaps more worrisome than these more commonly feared discoveries was the strange theater of sorrow to which I subjected my mama on more than one occasion:

Making myself cry for sport.

Entering my room unannounced, Mama would find me clutching a Barbie and sobbing bitterly, laid out on the floor. Ken had fled the shoebox apartment; Barbie had been left all alone.

"What the hell kind of game is this?" Mama asked, horrified.

How could I tell her I was indulging in grief fantasy?

Sometimes, I'd think upon the people I loved the most—Daddy, or Mama, or perhaps the baby squirrel. I'd meditate upon the things about them I treasured: Daddy's gravelly voice and the way he turned my name into art, Mama's long nails and elegant cigarettes and dark beauty, Fred's fluffy white belly and wiggling little nose. And then, one by one—I would imagine each of their deaths. Daddy gone, Mama gone, the squirrel gone—what would that feel like? I delighted to swim in this pain.

I don't remember my brothers getting in trouble for sex. Both of them were certainly active, my mama catching Michael on the receiving end of a blowjob in the basement one summer day; Jason chased relentlessly by school girls, indulging as he pleased. Nonetheless, I can't recall a single screaming match or crying jag that stemmed from my brothers' rendezvous.

The warning the world gave my brothers was this: *Don't you dare get that girl pregnant.*

The warning the world gave me was this: *Don't you dare be a whore.*

The dick in my mouth wasn't my first sexual transgression.

Months earlier, Mama had caught me with a hickey on my neck after a supposed girls' slumber party. She demanded of me, cigarette in her trembling hand, "was it everything you expected?"

"Yes," I lied.

And he wasn't even the first.

Before that, I'd lost my virginity to a neighborhood boy no older than me, a kid high on Christianity of the hand-waving, crying-in-church variety. Like me, he was physically precocious: a child wielding an adult's body. We weren't ready for ourselves, much less each other. Nonetheless, I noticed the way he watched me. Felt his eyes travel across my body.

So this is power.

I set out to abuse it.

4

Each bus ride to and from school, I'd cross and uncross my legs, hypnotizing him with a spell I didn't understand, inciting within him a longing he couldn't name. He French-kissed me at the bus stop, leaving crumbs from a PopTart on my chin. *So this is love.* Later, we went on a bike ride through the woods together, taking a break on a sunny patch to fumble with each other's bodies.

Although I couldn't imagine anything larger than a pinky inside me—and trust me, I'd tried—I nonetheless wanted this. Wanted to be grown. Wanted to be a woman. Wanted the stakes in my life to exceed tears shed over a Barbie or a heart wrapped up in a squirrel. When he fingered the button on my jeans, I welcomed the opportunity. Yet as before me he knelt, pants around his knees, I couldn't comprehend his body— otherworldly, a stranger. Different than the flat part between Ken's legs. Different than the drawings on the bathroom wall. Alive. Animal. I opened my knees to accept this foreigner.

I don't remember the pain of this, my first penetration—a lack of physical suffering for which I've felt forever guilty.

What I do remember: the clear blue sky above me, the buzz of a mosquito in my ear. My hair pinned beneath his hand. He thrust once, twice, thrice, and four, and then leapt from me as if stung by a wasp. Turning his back to me, he shuddered into the leaves.

As I puzzled over whether this actually counted—how many seconds does it take to make sex?—he dropped his head into his hands and sunk down upon a tree stump. He curled into himself, wrapping his arms around his legs. I wanted those arms wrapped around *me*.

From within the fortress he'd built of his body, I heard a hiccup. A sob. Weeping.

"What's the matter?" I asked.

"I've betrayed my earthly father," he answered, "and I've betrayed my heavenly father, as well."

I'd shuddered nothing into the leaves. Of course, no girl had any such right. But what about his arms around me afterward? Did I stand to gain nothing from this dance in the dirt?

Instead, I was a poison potent enough to offend both man and God.

"Get on your bike," I spat. "We're going home."

My daddy had not been brought up with gentleness. When he was a boy, his mother murdered a nest of baby birds for the crime of singing. Also, his father busted open the head of a sick kitten with a rock because he didn't want to pay for a vet. My daddy was only eight years old when he witnessed his father brain that cat. Daddy told me these stories just as matter-of-fact as a grocery list.

You'd think in all this hardness, not an inch of tenderness could bloom.

Yet, Fred was as tame as a cat when Daddy was around.

But—when Daddy was gone—

That squirrel went wild.

I grew up under my mama's people. My daddy's people actually *ate* squirrel. So when Daddy's mama died a few weeks after we rescued Fred, I stayed home while Daddy's family gathered for her funeral.

On that day, I had the house to myself for once, and that meant I had Fred to myself for once, too.

I opened the cage and held my palm by the door, expecting the rascal to step as gingerly into my hand as I'd seen him step so often into Daddy's.

But instead, he flew.

Across the den in a flash, Fred soared.

Onto the cupboard in the dining room, Fred leapt.

Weaving through porcelain teacups, landing on fine saucers, orchestrating a cacophony of shattering china, Fred played.

Treating Mama's finest dishes like trees in a forest, the squirrel sprung from perch to perch. Mama's nice things crashed to pieces around my feet while Fred enjoyed life to the fullest.

I would get in trouble for this.

I spent the morning panicked, trying to corral this animal. First, I tried the soft whistle that always worked for Daddy. Fred ignored that. Next, I removed my shirt and flung it at him. Fred was too fast for my makeshift net. Finally, my cheeks hot with tears, I lay on the floor still as death, palms open, hoping he would simply step into my hand. Yet atop Mama's corner cupboard, Fred perched, content, immune to my plans.

This was how Daddy found me when he returned home from burying his mother: shirtless in a training bra and weeping on the floor with my palms open in surrender, broken dishes all around.

"Fred went wild," I said.

On the cupboard, happily licking his paws, Fred took a breather in the gravy boat.

Although at the time I didn't appreciate the gravity of burying a parent—though soon I would—I realize now that my daddy probably had worse things on his mind than a runaround squirrel. Nonetheless, with seriousness he stuck out his hand, patient, like waiting on the rain, and whistled one quick whistle.

And just like that, Fred hopped into his palm.

Daddy could speak to birds, too, you know—could hold entire conversations with the forest.

Sometimes, I thought he was one of the wild things himself.

Sometimes, I thought I might be, too.

When I was five, my mama gave me my first diary. That year, I would begin a chronicle of my youth that would stretch into adulthood that had at the heart of every entry my obsessions with a revolving door of boys, the greatest goal of my life, gaining their favor.

As grade school turned into junior high, Mama taught me how to achieve beauty.

Taking me in the bathroom, sitting me on the counter, pulling my shirt over my head, she'd inform me that my breasts, while small, would have a nice shape—and my eyes— dark serious pools of mahogany—would cast spells. "It's in the blood," Mama told me, a black magic charm, a natural born legacy. As puberty rounded the corner, turning the flat plains of my body into a fraught territory of mountains and caves that terrified and thrilled us both, Mama trained me on how best to weaponize my assets.

"What's that boy you like, the one from Forest Hills?" she asked, as she plucked hairs from my brows, tears popping into my eyes. "You'll get his attention now."

At thirteen, my latest obsession was a prominent member of the Forest Hills gentry, a boy whose pedigree deemed him desirable by the tastemakers of John M. Langston Junior High. I wonder now—when those kids' parents purchased their nice homes along the tree-lined streets well out of the view of Danville's smokestacks, did they understand the extent of what they were buying for their children?

I hated my folks for moving us to the country. Our phone number revealed our lesser station. Anybody giving out digits beginning in 822- had good reason to be ashamed.

"Can you at least put me in dance?" I begged Mama, knowing full well that all the best-liked girls in Danville attended Martha Folke's Dance Academy.

"Absolutely not."

Dance was for the good families—

And we hated the good families.

However, after my Forest Hills crush held my hand in the hallway at school, my stock began to rise. I started receiving invitations to birthday parties I'd never known existed. It felt good to belong. I would do whatever it took to solidify my new station.

And so, as I knelt before that boy on that fateful afternoon, I was determined to secure his continuing admiration.

But suddenly, the bedroom door slammed open.

And there—stood Daddy.

That face that had smiled so sweetly upon an orphaned squirrel, those eyes that had danced with pride at my artistic strivings—now closed into one hard line. There were no words, only disgust.

Palpable.

His little girl?

No.

That was the moment I lost him.

I scrambled to my feet—but there was no hiding what I'd done.

Daddy lunged into my room and grabbed my boyfriend by the shoulders. He dragged him down the stairs and kicked him square in the ass out the door.

I loved this boy whose dick I'd been sucking. I was sucking his dick for love. Of all the boys who'd touched me in my thirteenth year, only this one had the bravery to call me his, only this one was willing to hold the hand of a nobody from the 822. As from my bedroom window, I watched my father drive that boy from our home back to the good neighborhood, my heart dropped. *I'll never see him again. They'll take him away from me.* I fancied us a modern Romeo and Juliet, with a vast and forbidden love whose forced dissolution would lead us both to death.

But it only led one of us to death.

"Don't you dare get that girl pregnant," my boyfriend's mother warned him when my daddy arrived with her son. She took away his phone privileges for a week.

At home, I found a different type of punishment awaiting me.

"You were giving him a blowjob, weren't you?" Mama flicked her cigarette hard, ash landing on the floor, every inch of her furious.

"You will *never* see him again. You will *never* have another boyfriend again. You will *never* leave your room again. You will *never* be happy again."

I knew I'd taken it too far. Yet I didn't know where to stop. I didn't know where the good seduction ended, the stuff that got you loved—and the bad seduction began, the stuff that got you hated. Why did we pluck my eyebrows if not for this success?

"You're crying?" she asked. "Good. You should be crying."

And then—Daddy reentered our home.

I looked to him. This man who plastered my name across walls. This man who spoke to the birds. This beloved daddy who unbeknownst to any of us had only three years left to live. I looked to him to intervene.

And he—looked away.

"I never wanted a whore for a daughter," he said, as he walked back out our door.

After Fred broke Mama's good dishes, Daddy decided it was time for him to go.

"A squirrel belongs in the woods," he said, opening the cage.

With his usual friendliness, Fred hopped right into Daddy's hand. Wrapping his broad fingers around this featherweight creature, Daddy lifted Fred to his face, eyed up his sweet little paw, his thin round ears, his happily chattering mouth. Fred stood on his hind legs and stretched out to nuzzle his nose against Daddy's.

As together we knelt on our storm-watching porch, Fred comfortable in Daddy's palm for the final time, I saw a tear drop from my father's eye. He rubbed the tear into the squirrel's fur and lowered him to the ground. Fred put one paw on the grass—testing—and then another. And then, just as quickly as he'd appeared in our lives weeks earlier, he now disappeared, speeding across the yard and scaling the magnolia as if he'd never fallen out of it.

"I'm worried about him being so high up," I told Daddy as we watched Fred climb.

"Don't. He was born for this."

But I could tell by the way Daddy lingered outside, staring upwards into the branches, that he was worried, too.

I rummaged in the kitchen cabinets until I found a bottle of sleeping pills.

I poured myself a large glass of Mama's sweet tea.

I sat on my bed and emptied the pills into my palm, munching mouthfuls like candy.

Next, I penned a garbled suicide note that pleaded for absolution from everybody from Jesus, to my parents, to Fred the squirrel.

Most of what happens next is fuzzy. I wrote my boyfriend's initials across my stomach. I painted my face—blue eye shadow, red lipstick, streaks of pink across my cheeks. Too much. Too much of everything. I am too much of everything and I am the only girl in the world sucking dick.

And then: the weight of sleep upon me, a blanket by the fire on a snowy day, irresistible. Sinking in. How easy it is to die.

Sometime afterward, Mama rushed into my room. She would later say she was compelled by a magical force to scale the stairs with a speed not her own, to pop the lock with a strength not hers. When she threw the door open at last and found me lifeless on the bed with a suicide letter by my side, she bellowed, long and low, *David!*

As the ambulance sped through my neighborhood, a friend of mine followed along. She arrived at my home to find me strapped to a board, head lolling, carried on the shoulders of men in uniform.

"Is she going to be okay?" she asked a paramedic.

"No," he replied, loading me in.

My daddy stood on the steps, this friend would later tell me, frozen and silent, my suicide note folded in his hand. When she asked him what had happened, he could only answer,

"She's sick. She's sick."

Hours later I awoke, strapped to a hospital bed, lurching black sludge all over Granny Audrey's dress as she waited by my bedside for signs of life.

"I have to pee!" I yelled between fits of vomiting.

"That's been taken care of," a nurse advised me.

I had been catheterized.

My stomach had been pumped.

I had been strapped down.

I lived.

I survived myself.

What humiliation.

I was locked in the psych ward for a week, making paper flowers and drawing hand turkeys and smoking cigarettes handed out by orderlies. I asked Jesus to save me from what awaited when I returned home—the wrath of my parents, the prying eyes of my peers, the fall from the esteem I'd so briefly enjoyed. What boy would ever hold my hand in the hallway now?

When I returned home, Mama wouldn't look at me. Daddy stopped writing my name. But they never stopped attending my brothers' baseball games. Why was I alone so wholly untouchable? I never asked. I was learning the order of things.

At school, the Algebra teacher advised my classmates to refrain from indulging me. "This is attention-seeking behavior," she warned. In the hallway, boys elbowed one another when I passed, laughing. The girls drove their eyes to the floor. "Mother says I can't be your friend anymore."

I had only wanted to belong, but instead I had turned myself invisible.

I decided then: I will turn this scarlet letter into a rifle on my shoulder.

And listen—I was devoted. I won't beg for love. I don't need my daddy. I don't need my mama. I don't need a friend, not a single one. All those years practicing tragedy had prepared me for this moment. I'll be your whore. I'll be your whore in vibrant colors all across this shitty town. Pour into me everything you hate about you. I accept it. I want it. I know now who I am.

As soon as it was legal, I hit the strip club stage.

CHAPTER TWO

Too Pretty To Be Good

"Are you studying?" Mama asked, the worry palpable in her voice despite the one hundred and forty-four miles I'd put between us. A half-day's drive through tobacco fields and a world away from Evilland, I skipped college composition, painted my face, and lied to my mama.

"Of course I'm studying," I said, balancing the phone on my shoulder, rotating an eyeliner over a lighter's flame. Softening the crayon, rolling the pencil between my fingers, a moving meditation: you want the darkness to spread with ease.

Outside my window, the setting sun crept through the fire escapes that dotted Richmond, Virginia, painting the town in stripes of shadow. Somewhere, in the darkest corner of this city, where abandoned warehouses moldered, suspicious persons crept, and a neon naked lady shone into the night, my first shift at a strip club awaited.

"I've got to do something about these dark circles," I complained to Mama as I studied my face.

"Well, you *do* look just like my daddy," she reminded me.

Those of us who bear the mark of Walter Shelton carry a certain darkness into the lightest of events—these black eyes, that heavy brow, a silent hurricane that churns the energy in even the most carefree of summer cook-outs, a storm of intensity generations in the making. It's in the blood, Mama tells me, taking me into her bedroom whenever the chance arises, holding up a five-by-eight in sepia tones, the frame worn to slickness with handling, a grandfather I never met flashing a smile as familiar as a mirror from beneath that moody gaze. His absence made a home in Mama's chest like an ogre under a bridge, reaching up to pull down any passers-by.

When Mama birthed my brother a few short years before her father left this world, he called the hospital, hopes high. "Does that baby look like me?" he asked.

A man as pretty as Walter Shelton couldn't help but be vain.

"No, Daddy," Mama laughed, "this baby don't look a thing like you."

But when I was born, it only took Mama one look to realize: *this child has my father's face.* And so, upon my arrival, she wept—not with joy, as most new mothers do—but with sadness. I was born too late, you see, her daddy dead and gone before he ever got the chance to see himself in me.

"It's not that he was a bad man," Granny Audrey has remarked of her first husband, from time to time. "He was just—too pretty to be good."

Mama hadn't wanted me to leave Danville. Her hair still white from my suicidal antics, her skin ashen from her own heart attack that followed, Mama finally lost her mind altogether for the remainder of the nineteen hundreds when Daddy died.

Daddy got sick, which was unusual because he was a man who could not be felled. When he missed work for two days, Mama knew something was wrong—perhaps the flu? A trip to the doctor—and then to the hospital—and then an emergency helicopter ride to Duke later, and Daddy was a hundred miles away by the time I came home from a sleepover early the next morning. As I walked through the front door, I found Mama standing on the stairs, frozen. "Your daddy's got leukemia," she said, just as flat out as if she were telling me it was going to rain that day, and then she promptly folded to her knees.

During the time of his dying, I found my mother's diary. Among entries of chemo dates and prognoses, I discovered scrawled large across a page, *I WANT OUR LIFE BACK.*

She never got it back.

That raven-haired beauty with the red nails and dark eyes turned to ash, clutching a photograph of her dead husband and sitting silent in his chair. She was only forty-three then. There was no room for me to lose my own mind, so vast was Mama's sadness, so hungry, so jealous. I wanted to bellow for my daddy, the one who had loved me with such tenderness and left with such suddenness, the one whose love I'd forfeited with my depravity; I wanted to rip open my chest and dig through my entrails to find what viscera were his—to hold, bloody, a piece of the man I'd never have back: here, this heart that loves storms, *this* is him; these lungs that breathe lightning, *these* are him; and now I shall feed these organs, pulsating and hot, into the dirt.

But I knew better than that.

A home can only hold so many black holes.

And so, as Mama imploded, I shattered outward.

At the age of sixteen, I was orphaned not once but twice, thrust suddenly into a freedom born of abject grief. Nobody was watching me anymore. Who had the heart-space for a wild girl? A lifetime of straight-As devolved into Fs, but nobody cared, least of all me. I could spend the night with grown men if I wanted.

My brothers showed up for Daddy's funeral, and then promptly returned to the lives they'd created since they'd moved away. I alone remained in Evilland, occupying a home heavy with the presence of Daddy's absence, a carton of Marlboros forever unsmoked on the kitchen counter, a tube of Alizarin Crimson leaking on his easel, dust collecting on the paint like a cloud across a sunrise. I alone remained with Mama in that house that had once held three people, but now held two and a closet full of clothes for a dead man. Daddy's lunchbox became Mama's child then. She paced the house cradling his left-behind things while I raced out the door.

That house was haunted, but not by Daddy. He died and I haven't heard from him since.

It was the year 2000. I was nineteen, a college freshman and recent Danville escapee, not so much tasting freedom as devouring it whole. I'd spent my girlhood watching boys win trophies—where I'm from, women play supporting roles; we occupy bleachers. Not me, not anymore. If my brothers could leave Danville, so could I. College provided the perfect excuse, a degree in English the natural course for a girl who got off on Edgar Allen Poe. I spent my free time composing poems—coffins on beaches, corpses, birds squawking doom in your ear.

"You ought not be so goddamned dark," Mama told me, handing back a journal of poetry she'd dug from my closet.

The failing grades that followed Daddy's death might have kept me from the top universities my peers were attending—as with packed bags and smiling parents, one by one classmates embarked upon freshman year. However, one school did accept my application, despite the ugliness of my senior grades—Virginia Commonwealth University in Richmond. Along with my acceptance into college, in turn I accepted loans bigger than any money I'd ever seen. "They're just giving *thousands* away," I told Mama, wonder in my voice.

And so, when I started stripping, I can't say I needed the money. I had Uncle Sam's borrowed cash in the bank.

No, it wasn't money I needed.

What I needed—was vindication.

What a reversal I would pull upon my enemies!

And that's how, just few days after leaving Danville, I journeyed into the shadowy labyrinth of Richmond's warehouse district and walked into my first strip club.

A half-orphan, the town slut, unlovable by all. The one the boys liked enough to touch, but not enough to claim. Hands clasped in the dark of closets but not in the hallway at school. Did you know you can get paid for touching boys in closets?

On my first night ever stripping, I destroyed my car.

I say "my car," and I suppose technically it was, but the vehicle had in fact belonged to Daddy. Evidence of him was everywhere. The upholstery, once grey, wa stained brown from cigarette smoke; a grease stain in the shape of his palm forever marked the glove box. But perhaps most poignantly to me, a ping-pong ball with a smiley face rolled around the interior of the vehicle, the face drawn in Daddy's hand.

When somebody dies, it's the details you miss, the roughness of the palm, the blackness of the nail, a pack of paint gathering dust on an easel, a face drawn on a ball—these precious things announcing, *Look! Not long ago I was here, alive, carefree, and now—now I am nothing.*

I had a lot on my mind.

My drive to my first shift was harried, unfocused. After a rushed shopping spree at the stripper store, high on the purchase of a spandex pantsuit and six-inch pumps, I sped toward Club Hot Styxx—

And drove full-speed into the car stopped in front of me.

My hood crumpled with a crunch.

An old man climbed out of his stricken car to inspect the damage—only a dent for him. As he approached my car, I turned on the charm, smiled pretty. Just one block ahead, close enough that I could walk to it, awaited the strip club.

"Men love a Southern accent," Mama had always advised.

"I'm fixin' to go up yonder for an appointment," I crooned, "so if we could handle this real quick, I'd sure appreciate it, honey...."

He looked at me, confused.

"Are you hurt?" he asked, inspecting my face, frowning in concern.

"Why, no—I'm just fine!"

My hand fluttered to my cheek to search for blood, for wound, for injury.

Instead, beneath my fingers, I found tears.

As I lurched my battered car into the parking lot of Hot Styxx, beneath my foot an object crunched. Perhaps part of the dashboard had fallen in the wreckage, was rolling around the floorboard?

I parked the car and looked for the offending object.

Beneath my foot I found not a broken piece of the Honda, not a piece of garbage, not collision debris. Instead, I found a single ping-pong ball, smiling at me in the precious hand of my father, half-crushed by in my haste to get here.

That car and everything in it were all I had left of him.

I sailed past the goons flanking the front door and up the stairs to the dressing room, hoping I'd have time to gather my nerves. Come eight o' clock, all dancers were expected on the floor; one minute later would get you a fine.

The dressing room announced its presence through the nose first, waves of Exclamation perfume mingled with burning Newports. As I crossed the threshold into this unfamiliar lair, around me naked women surrounded mirrors, preening. Towering above everyone else in the room, her hair a golden mane, her eyes creased at the corners but nonetheless painted with the artful care of a veteran hoe, sat a regal individual, spine straight. Unlike most of us, this woman was no kid. The pride of her posture, the upward tilt of her chin, the way the others smiled brightly in her face and whispered behind her back, alerted me: this one here is the queen.

"Honestly, Babygirl," she muttered as I walked by, "what's with the pantsuit?"

Before I could answer, she pulled a trunk from beneath the makeup counter. Spray-painted on it were the words, "Sheena DO NOT TOUCH." Diving elbow-deep into a mass of garters and thongs, she reemerged at last with a sequined two piece. "A little sparkle," she said, handing it to me.

I stared at her offering, unsure if this woman I'd just met actually intended for me to wear her thong.

I'd been in rooms with naked girls before—after gym class, or at a pool party. In those spaces, however, we crouched over our bodies, backs curved and protective like turtle shells, pulling one shirt over the other before removing the first, threading bras through the arms of tees—afraid of our own bodies, afraid of each other's.

"Go ahead," Sheena urged, shoving her bikini into my hands. "Put it on."

And so I did.

As she fastened her top around my ribcage, she nodded toward the mirror.

"Tell me, Babygirl—what do you see?"

Flesh. Supple and full, straining the strings of the bikini. Breasts, newly-bloomed and high. Black-rimmed eyes. Red lips. A face painted with Wet N' Wild and inexactitude, a woman's art practiced with a child's hand. At my feet, the Norton's Anthology of American Literature peeked from my bookbag, my supposed-life in a pile on the floor. I kicked it under the dressing room counter, spun in the mirror and grinned. Of all the boys that had touched me, of the all men with whom I'd laid, never had anyone made me feel like a woman the way Sheena did that night.

She stepped back, hands on hips, scanning my body, examining her handiwork.

"Remind me again what your name is?"

"Lindsay."

"No, not your real name. Your stripper name."

"Oh. Lux."

"Lux! Where'd you get that?"

"Well, it's Latin for—"

"Whoa, kid, whoa. That ain't gonna work. These men don't want no damn Latin."

"Well, how about…luxury? Do they want luxury?"

"Babygirl, you *are* luxury. That's your story and you're sticking to it."

Clad in Sheena's bikini, I scanned the floor, hands sweaty and plans big. The air curled with smoke. Richmond, Virginia: we're in tobacco country now. Everybody in the world smokes here. Women in six-inch heels stalked the floor like Amazons through the jungle, eyes sharp for prey. In this dark corner, or that shadowy enclave, huntresses camouflaged in fishnet and neon—or nothing at all—stroked men's arms and egos, smiling and nodding their way into small fortunes. How gentle the kill. Beneath the flickering light of a neon PBR sign, one of these towering goddesses rose from a table, taking a man by the hand, leading him into a darker room, a place we all want to go, but for different reasons. Money. Power. Excitement. Validation. Whose desires are whose?

Among the swirling whirlpool of wants and needs that had driven me to this place, one desire now dominated my heart: I wanted to be an Amazon, too. I wanted my hands bloodied green with tender that would prove I'd won—never mind that I couldn't quite identify what battle I was fighting. The dark years of cruel laughter and rescinded invitations had been a steady march towards this fate, each wound another brick in the construction of me.

No one gave me a tour of Hot Styxx. No one gave me lessons.

I don't remember much about that night: a blur of electric nerves and ill-gained White Zinfandel, a man my professor's age inviting me into the dark room, running his broad hands over my body, the first of many hands that would caress me that night—so many men, none of them children, like me. On couches: women riding men. Men laid back in pleasure, haloes of steam dotting the mirrors behind them. A tall blonde, a statuesque marvel all legs and implants, balanced on a couch, her spiked heels sinking into the upholstery, her crotch pressed against the face of a skeletal dotard, the grim reaper himself inhaling fecundity.

"Let's sit," Professor of the Roving Hands told me, gesturing to an empty spot amidst this Caligulan pandemonium.

I don't know what to do with this man—but then again, I do. I do what I've done in basements, in locked bedrooms, in the backseat of cars, with boys I desired. I ride this man, whom

I don't desire, but I can still find the right spot with my thigh. I untied the knot of Sheena's top and let it drop.

"You stupid kid!"

With sudden ferocity, an old woman appeared from nowhere and jerked me up. A Pall Mall perched on her lip, she sunk her nails into my flesh.

Meet Mama, the housemom.

"You can't take off your goddamned top during a dance!" she hissed. "Didn't they teach you anything?"

And that's how, just one hour into my first shift, I earned my first strip club fine.

Of all the memories I possess of this, my night of initiation, I remember not the face of the professor, nor the faces of any of the men who would follow. Yet clearly I remember the crisscross lines beneath Mama's eyes, the way they led like crooked country roads to the firepit of her pupils. I was afraid of the heat in those eyes, the power, the rage against stupid kids like me.

I paced the dressing room, my cheeks burning with humiliation.

"That's probably a sixty-dollar mistake," Sheena surmised. She cocked one leg up on the make-up counter, pulled her thong to the side, and inserted a tampon. With a pair of scissors, she snipped the string a hair's breadth from her flesh, tucking the rest inside.

"You want my advice, Babygirl? Set a goal. Walk in thinking, I've got to make four hundred dollars tonight. At twenty dollars a dance, that's twenty dances."

"Four hundred dollars?"

"Four hundred is what you want to *clear*, Babygirl—you've gotta *make* a lot more than that. The house, the DJ, the bouncers, the housemom—every one of 'em will have a hand out at the end of the night. So go ahead and add another ten dances to that twenty. And one last thing, kid—lose the frown. There ain't no such thing as a frown in a titty bar."

She massaged her fingers into her cheeks.

I'd soon know this pain, the soreness of smiling without end, the knot in your jaw that spreads like a strap beneath your chin, a muscle cramped tight to shut up complaints and replace them with quiet loveliness.

"Sit down and ask him, right off the bat: 'How do you feel about corny jokes?' Everybody likes corny jokes. Then tell him this:

"'What did the egg say to the boiling water?'

"I don't know, what.

"It said, 'It might take me a while to get hard, I just got laid.'

"Then—hit him with the sale.

"When you grind, grind him slow. Only pick up the pace as the song ends. When he asks what you'll do when you get home tonight—they always do—tell him: *masturbate*.

"What you'll really do when you get home tonight: feast upon a peanut butter sandwich."

She turned in the mirror for a final inspection. Bending over, she spread her cheeks, checking for any loose string that might betray her blood, her messy humanity. "Get hard," she told me, over her shoulder. "Most these motherfuckers ain't gonna want you."

Do you like corny jokes

"I just got back from the golf course," answered the red-faced accountant. "Been here fifteen minutes and I still haven't seen a waitress. Where's the goddamn waitress?"

What did the egg say to the boiling water

"I don't know," said the loudest of the three car salesmen, "what did the boss say to his employees? He says I closed four sales this week, and that's why I'm the fucking boss!"

It might take me a while to get hard

A man in sunglasses beckoned me to his table and then ignored me completely, engrossed in sports TV.

I just got laid

Trucker placed a cigarette deep within his beard, put his hand in mine. "It's hard to have a lover on the road," he told me, "hard to find love when you're putting it in the wind." He pulled me into his chest, breathing me in. On his clothes I could smell weeks of wear. In his arms, I could feel years of yearning. I rode him in the back until he was spent.

Afterwards, I locked myself in the bathroom and stood before the mirror. I pulled my breasts from my top and squeezed them luxuriously. I was born for this. Bred for this. Red lips, black hair, the supple skin of a newborn woman, the black knowledge drawn from a youth observing beauty queens, a teenage nightmare casting spells in the dark—all the puzzle pieces needed to win this game, already I possessed. Running my hands down my body, I grinned at my reflection. A million men can touch me tonight—I don't care. In the mirror, I am mine.

As my taxi rolled away from Hot Styxx, I watched Daddy's crumpled car disappear into the darkness and counted what I had earned: one hundred and eighty-six dollars. Without the fine, it would've been well over two hundred. I grinned; counted again.

A fortune, I marvelled—a fortune.

I am worth so fucking much.

CHAPTER THREE
Starving

When it comes to men, the women in my family have a great need.

Loving them, begging them, mourning them: these are our ways.

The more elusive the man, the better upon which to thrash your heart: we only give ourselves to those who turn away, who tire of our lilting step, our coy smile, our string of yesses; the mark of a good man, his rejection: ain't nobody that wants me nobody worth having.

"Every woman should have at least one good love story," Mama always said, but to Mama, a love story meant blood and tears, diamond rings flung across the front yard, agony and destruction. "He'll squander your love with a floozie in a pool hall," she laughed. I imagined her at twenty-one, bouncing my brother, then an infant, on her knee, staring out the window of their trailer, having bathed and fed the baby and scrubbed the tub and washed the clothes and now at last having a moment to think, to wonder where her husband was, where he'd been all night, to get used to the idea that he might stay gone for the whole day, or maybe even forever this time. Mama was starved to death by the time her husband's best friend came striding up to her door, looking for a meal.

That man would become my daddy.

The strip club stage is where I learned to dance, surrounded by mirrors and men at my feet. Sometimes those men would admire me, and the show would be for them. Sometimes they would ignore me, or simply not be there—a slow Tuesday— and the show would be for me. I remember watching myself move in those mirrors, thinking, *if only this were considered art, I'd have a legitimate talent.*

The way I looked under those lights, in those mirrors, was a feast among famine. I devoured my reflection. When I'd rise from a man after a dance, towering over him, my skin damp and burning, hand out for compensation, I tasted power. I can still see me, in those mirrors, in those early years, my smile glowing white under the black light, a star in a galaxy of darkness. How can light be black? Allow me to demonstrate with my existence. Flowing hair sewn tight against my scalp, plump breasts, round tummy, legs long and thick at the thighs, a shapeshifter you wouldn't recognize in the grocery store. There's an art to becoming this woman. I have been conjuring this woman all the moonlit nights of my life.

I'm a stripper, I'd tell anyone who asked, from the greasy-haired clerk at the gas station, to the girl behind the make-up counter at Macy's. "I need a blush that shimmers," I told the sales lady—"*for the stage.*" She smiled politely and fetched Summer Sun. A thrill rushed through my veins: *fuckin'-A, I'm telling people this shit.* I'd call it a confession, if it weren't a boast.

It was hard to say whether what I was doing was right or wrong, during those dark hours in downtown Richmond, my nights a frenzy of physical gyrations and emotional machinations, collapsing finally at four a.m. in a dark apartment thick with my roommate's sleep, my whole self languid with the delicious pain of my bruised and bleeding body, trembling, scalded in a shower. My plans to attend class in the morning spiraled down the drain with the smell of men's cologne. It was hard to say whether what I was doing was wrong or right, but I knew well enough to hide the crinkled cash from my roommate's boyfriend, had heard him from behind the closed door of her bedroom ask, *I thought y'all were here to go to school?* Yet as she continued to attend class, I continued to sleep in.

Have you ever felt the drugged heaviness of the sleep-deprived, have you pulled beneath your chin the hundred-pound blanket that muffles wake-up calls like a silencer on a shotgun? Seductive, opioid, quicksand, that bed, those cool sheets tangled around your legs, the hot sun crawling silently across the bedroom.

It was hard to say whether what I was doing was right or wrong—but I certainly did wonder, in the afternoons of my waking, my neck wet with sweat, the blankets a pile on the floor.

Before I left Danville, the combined stigma of my suicide attempt, known promiscuity, and dead parent established me among my peers a pariah too strange and terrible to engage. All the boys for whom I'd cheered from the sidelines remained absent at Daddy's funeral: a slight I would grasp with the tenacity of a wild dog to a bone. Yet, an optimistic adventurer saw me and became enchanted.

He worked for the forestry department during summers, planting gypsy moth traps throughout rural Virginia. He was adept at navigating uncharted wilderness on compass alone. He cut his way through brambles with nothing more than a map and a machete. He took the hard route. He took me to prom when my boyfriend went to jail. He built furniture and befriended wild dogs. When I gave him my body as a thank you for his kindness—the best and only gift I knew how to give—he whispered, with each movement, "is this okay?" His generosity with me, I dimmed with calculated instigations, fights over the small things. Did he look at that girl in the mall? Did he breathe in a way that could insinuate an insult? How can there be love without pain? How can this be real if it doesn't shred me? In my family, love meant car horns sounded through the night, dramatic entrances wielding baseball bats, tears at a man's feet. Did you not hear about Mama's first marriage? Did you not hear how she ended up with Daddy? Did you not hear about Granny's first marriage? Tragedy runs in the family. We measure love in units of agony, beauty in the depth of the bruise.

Other boys had loved me. But they had only loved with a half-way love. Love hidden in basements when their mama wasn't home. Love given in the woods behind school and revoked in the hallway. Love, an open hand closed into a fist. Given. Taken away. Nothing one could savor. Nothing one could count on.

But this boy's kindness knew no limit. Therefore, I could not understand nor accept his love. In turn, he tried to jump off a roof.

My heart was a well without end, a black hole ripping to pieces those who travelled too close. I had become so difficult that I had caused a good boy to go crazy. That's how potent my poison. Just like I had caused Mama to have a heart attack. I saw with my own eyes her hair turn white in the single year between my near-death encounter and her own.

A cloud of discord followed me, kicked up by my scramble over the rocks of my life.

That cloud became my identity.

Trouble followed me, and that's how I liked it.

Might as well like it.

I took to wearing dog collars with spikes.

"This job will ruin you for men," Sheena told me one night, a few months into my new life—months that carried a gravity of influence usually only possessed by years, decades, eras. I was changed already by the Styxx, was changing still. Sheena rolled the charms of her bracelet between her fingers, passing the initials of each of her children through her hand like a rosary.

"Even the ones that actually care about you," she said.

"Please don't hurt me," he begged, as with the tenderest fury he bent the metal frame of my futon, driving his body into me, his hipbones painting bruises onto my thighs. We had only just met, strangers at a kegger, drawn to the hunger in one another's eyes. He was blonde, fresh, and too beautiful for this world, a broken bowl with golden cracks. I was dark, a cave that begs exploration. We were children, starved, wailing into the night.

"Y'all be quiet!" my roommate yelled from behind her bedroom door.

Bill was brought up in the backwoods of Ohio, a quiet blue-eyed boy that fetched beers at parties while his mama danced on the hood of the car and his daddy got madder and madder. He was an angel getting dirty in the backwoods of Earth. His parents broke up; Daddy called Mommy a cunt; Daddy shot the family dog; Bill moved to Richmond. He was a runaway like me, pretty and wounded.

In the beginning, he allowed the stripping, because in the beginning, one allows certain things. I didn't want to admit that the only person I found as intoxicating as Bill was Lux—didn't want to own that: not to him, not to me. There was already crime in a girl loving herself—that was vanity. Double the crime dare she love herself, body spilling from sequins, face painted like a whore. No mortal man could compete with the mythical apparition I became after an hour at the make-up counter. To set his beauty against my own in a deathmatch for my love would mean murder to both warring angels. I couldn't afford to lose either. And so I played the "I need the money" card, I played the "I will only do this for a few months" card, not knowing then that these excuses would become a permanent fixture in how I bargained for love from men all the days of my life.

The narcotic of my body, pliable in his arms, the nectar of my admiration, the ringing of our laughter as wrapped in sheets we chased each other around my room, pretending to be ghosts: these treasures protected him for a time from the sharp edges of my existence. I knew some aspects of me hurt him. I wanted to salve his wounds, not peel them open. So we didn't talk about my work.

He would arrive at my apartment mid-day between pizza deliveries, smelling of oregano and a beat-up Pontiac, wrap his arms around me and close his lips on my throat, my pulse in his mouth, my life pounding against his tongue. His fingers are long and his face is delicate and his beauty is his woundedness; he takes the legs out from under me; my aching body, now soothed into drugged satiation under his touch. We can't make it to the couch, much less the bed. He makes love to me on the floor in the afternoon, and returns in the evening for dinner. I swallow his love with the greedy selfishness of one who hasn't eaten in days. Weeks. Years. I can't remember my last meal. I want our love to last forever.

Like everything else, it would not.

"I'm going to marry this man," I told my mama, breathless, over the phone.

"Here's hoping," she replied.

But a golden-haired guitar picker too beautiful for this world cannot wade in a woman made of earth.

Water becomes whatever you pour it into. Be like water.

"Bruce Lee taught me that."

Sheena poured my beer into an empty wine glass. "You'd just 'bout think this was champagne now," she continued, pointing to the golden bubbles filling the flute.

When closing time arrived, Sheena changed. She removed three rows of clip-in hair, her crown deflating. She took off her lashes with a tug and stuck them to the mirror, two terrible centipedes marking her spot. Sheena meant something here. She could claim a spot in this crowded dressing room, where other women fought for corners and settled for seats on the floor. "Sheena is our top earner," the owner announced during one of his monthly visits, a broad-chested bastard with a cigar in one hand and our fates in the other. Sheena stroked his wide arm and shrunk two feet in size, tiny, adoring, gazing up dumbly. Become like water—fill whatever shape you're poured into.

When Sheena's boyfriend came to pick her up at the end of the night, her back that usually ran straight and sharp curled like a potato bug. "Hurry the fuck up," he barked from his rattling truck, and she walked faster.

Ever since I ruined Daddy's car, I'd been begging rides to the club off friends. However, now that Bill had come into my life, he quickly became my chauffeur to the strip club. Anything to spend a few extra moments with him. This was not a gig he relished. He grew quiet when he dropped me off, our laughter dissolving into silence as we pulled into the parking lot. I squeezed his knee as I opened the car door, an attempt at a tickle that didn't take. Laugh, baby, laugh—so I know you will still love me despite what I am about to do.

Among the girls at work, there ran a certain wisdom: if your man doesn't let you strip, you don't let him be your man. Insecure, jealous, possessive, controlling—these were the judgments pinned upon those that tried to get between us and the job. Taking her friend's face in her hands, carefully wiping away smeared mascara, Mercedes told Chanel, "If he don't pay your bills, he don't get a say." Chanel swallowed hard and nodded.

But I wouldn't just kick to the curb *my* man. I loved him with an intensity that was absolutely fearful. I couldn't feel the sun on my shoulders as we strolled Carytown without his fingers interlaced in mine, could not taste ice cream savored alongside the James River without his tongue tasting first.

We tangled our bodies together in the heat of Indian summer for a homemade photo shoot, passing a bulky camera between us, a joint smoldering on his lip, a ray of sun silhouetting his profile as I drew him into focus. These photos, I treasure still, saved in a trunk my husband doesn't explore. *I* explore them, however, when I'm alone, now twenty years away from that day in September, with each secret visitation my heart pierced to discover just how lithe he was, how thin, cords of tendon and angle of bone and hollow of eye, a newborn man not yet fully fleshed. And me, nude, leaning against a door frame, cheeks plump with youth, my dark eyes speaking into the camera, into the eyes behind that lens, *thank you, thank you, thank you.*

"What you need is a regular."
Sheena plunked a stack of cash on the make-up counter.
"You're ready for it," she said. "You got that look."

"What look?"

"The look of someone that's in love."

"I *am* in love," I answered, eyes glazing over.

"I ain't talking 'bout no damn dude, Lux," she replied. "I'm talking about *you*. You—are in love with *you*."

So she'd seen it, then. So it could be witnessed, my rapture upon the stage. I wondered what it had been like for her, when she was my age. Had she come from an evil town built upon a previous generation's dead dreams? Had she spent her girlhood admiring pointed bras and long nails and cocked hips and the way those things earned everything worth earning? Her women, her kin—were they always pretty and pleasing while the men just had a good old time acting whichever way they chose? Had there ever been a time when this lioness with the mane of brass had worn her hair in a dirty braid, freckles splayed across her nose, unseen in the bleachers while her brothers hit line drives and saw their names run in the Danville Register and Bee? Had there ever been a time when this Amazonian huntress had stridden upon the stage a wobbly-kneed colt, braid brushed out and lipstick messy, heart frightened—and then filled—to discover in the mirror a woman she'd wanted all her life?

My daddy didn't just keep art in his workshop.

He hid pornography in there, too.

On the second shelf of his drafting table, beneath a cigar box of pencils, crammed within a Sears catalogue, I found his secret magazines. I don't remember the first time I discovered these treasures. Somehow, it seems like they were always there, their presence an open secret stashed beneath art supplies.

I knew for a fact those magazines were bad. One time, Mama caught me in Daddy's workroom with a Gallery mag spread open in my lap, and she was horrified. "Well!" she gasped, removing from my mitts the offending obscenity. "Daddy uses those for—his figure drawing!" She absconded to her room, magazine in hand, never to speak of this again.

But judging from Daddy's landscapes hanging throughout our home, I was the only one in this house drawing women.

From the closed door of Daddy's workroom, they beckoned to me: busty babes sporting tan lines and teased bangs, legs spread just enough, their eyes smiling, the spirit of *yes* on their lips. I wanted them. I wanted to *be* them. I could not name nor understand this yearning, yet I knew with a determination that ignores all consequence of sin—I had to get one of these magazines alone.

And so, when my parents left to run errands one day, I rushed to Daddy's workshop the moment their car left the driveway. I memorized the order of his stack of art things before invading. Removed the cigar box, gingerly—must not spill the pencils; must keep my presence here unknown. Holding the Sears catalogue by the spine, shaking gently the open pages towards the ground, the Gallery mag dropped to the floor. I snatched it and sped to my room.

If the desire for naked ladies wasn't bad enough, then even worse was the consummation of my mission.

In my room, I opened the magazine, laid on my belly as I perused. Eyes running over nipples, wooly valleys, pink lips, I pressed my face into the pages and my fist beneath my body. I'd like one day to be featured in this here magazine! Now wasn't that a thrilling thought! I gazed upon these grown women's bodies, picturing my own face atop them. The blood surged through me as I rocked against my hand, drawing a feeling I'd never felt before, electric and unstoppable. And it wasn't those naked ladies

I saw as my body caught pleasure forbidden, not their beautiful breasts, nor their faces, nor their bright teeth, their glossy lips, no. The face I saw when I came was my own.

"I know a man who might could sponsor you," Sheena told me, as side-by-side we strode the club floor.

Other dancers wondered why Sheena had taken me on. Befriended me. Been nice to me. I asked to borrow Mercedes' flat iron once and Mercedes barked back, "only Chanel can use my flat iron!" This was a place of factions, splinter cells, loyalties questioned and personal business guarded. I have known women's bodies by the inch and never known their real names. Familiarity did not always bring friendship. I remember walking into the dressing room, sweaty, a dollar stuck to my shoe, when Heaven looked up at me from her Caboodles on the floor, mean as hell. "Don't nobody think that wig is real," she spat, unprovoked.

I don't know if I'd call it friendship, what I had with Sheena. I desired her, and she must have felt that desire, probably from the first moment I'd seen her in the dressing room. She wasn't the first popular girl I'd longed for. Sure, we had the smart set in Danville—the Suburban Debutantes, they called themselves, or Sub-Debs for short—blondes for miles, trophies for the best boys of Forest Hills, pearls passed down from mother, Boone's Farm at the bonfire party. I always wanted an invite; I never got one. But now, I had Sheena. She was sharp where those girls had been round. To walk by her side made me proud.

I'd been working at the club long enough to know the basic protocol. Nine months, ten months, the better part of a year. I'd rode many a man for a twenty.

But I hadn't yet garnered a regular.

Lexie went to the outlet mall with her regular each Sunday the Lord sent. It was said that Alicia's sugar daddy had bought her a car. It was even rumored that some of these men would pay your rent. Some of them, it was said, would even put you on an allowance.

Sheena and I sidled up to the bar and watched the customers trickle in, the Styxx waking slow like a circus tent rising in a field.

"And what do they want out of this deal," I asked her, "these regulars?"

Expectations were already high at the lowest level of customer engagement: roving hands, chiding tone of voice if compliance you lacked, angry eyes that made you believe they'd paid for whatever they wanted of you. How might these terms ratchet even higher should you commit to a regular? What must it cost, for example, to accept a car from a man? The courtesy among us girls was not to ask.

"Some things, better to learn on your own," Sheena answered, scanning the crowd.

A regular is special. A regular isn't like other customers. You, of course, are Julia Roberts. He, of course, is Richard Gere. This, of course, is the game. The trap. Cultivate his love. Falsify feelings. Entertaining these men—ain't easy. You think emotion is endless, a stream that flows without end, ever more dazzling smiles and ringing laughter to come for forever and ever amen, until one late night or early morning—you can't tell the difference anymore—you creep into bed next to a man that you *do* love and yet you can't tap that love, not a single iota, can't touch his heart any more than you could touch the bottom of the sea. Your bounty has become a desert, and your man doesn't want a mouthful of sand. He'll tell you goodbye with his closed body for weeks, months, before he utters the horrible truth. You put your arms around him as you creep into his bed, and in response, he rolls away.

"He's here," Sheena smiled, as a man the shape of a mountain walked into the Styxx. "Your regular."

CHAPTER FOUR

She Fucked Up Up
Her Whole Yard

As night fell, I watched out my window for Fred, searching the labyrinth of the magnolia for movement, its branches tangled and wild against a black sky. Straining my eyes in the moonlight, I scanned the tree he'd alighted upon with such confidence that morning, wondering if that confidence remained now that night had fallen. What if he's stuck up there? Or worse—what if there was a hawk in that tree? Whatever cruel obstacle may await him, with dark certainty, I knew—no matter what God had intended for this tree-climbing creature, my hand-raised baby was no match for that magnolia, savage and two-faced, streaming sun through its flowers in the day, yet a gnarled ghoul in the night. Perhaps snakes coiled through its branches even now.

Below my window, the front door opened, streaming a bar of light from our home into the darkened yard. Into that ray of light entered my father. He was on his way to work—Daddy worked the third shift. Daddy's commitment to extreme work hours, sometimes sixty a week, was his prime point of pride— besides his art, of course. Daddy was usually in a hurry to get to Miller Brewing. However, on this night, something was different. Daddy wasn't in a hurry—I could tell by the way he set his lunchbox down and peered into that tree.

So unlike him, to waste time. So like him, to harbor a secret tenderness. He stood there a good few minutes, searching. And then he held out his hand and whistled.

Nothing.

As he picked up his lunchbox and set on toward his car, Daddy looked up behind him, to our home, to my bedroom window, where I sat, spying. For an instant, his eyes caught mine. I flung the curtain closed—not because I didn't want Daddy to catch me worrying over Fred—but because I didn't want him to catch me catching *him,* worrying right there along with me.

I walked into the Hot Styxx a teenager sporting lofty moral codes concocted in the space of hypothetical daydreaming, behavioral oaths that failed to correlate with the messiness of actual reality. I wouldn't do this; I wouldn't do that. High intentions, naïve ideals. Absolutes like "good" and "bad." That shit don't stack up in real life.

In the first few months on the job, you think no one else is nosy; you chide yourself for stealing glances at the other girls' numbers on the tip-out sheet, calculating in your mind algebraic equations that reveal the level to which you should resent, admire, or hate-lust the others. Goddamn, if Sheena tipped out five hundred to the DJ tonight, imagine the implications of her overall earnings. *This bitch.* I wanted to love her. I did love her. But her success made me hate her for about twenty-two white hot seconds as each night closed.

Now *that* was an esteem I yearned to obtain: a high number on the tip-out sheet. *That* was a position I craved: top girl in the house. A toxic desire, destined to mutate every cell of my body. Those whom I admired, now morphed into those I must dominate.

I trailed Sheena's footsteps, her white pumps beacons in the blacklight, leading me down darker and more twisting hallways than before, as we searched the club for my mark, the man she had decided would be my regular, a game of matchmaker unlike any other. Why she would aid me in this way, why she had taken me under her wing, I couldn't quite grasp, though I certainly appreciated the guidance.

"Do you know about this room," she asked, as she opened a door marked *private*. Behind that door, a miniature club awaited, a single pedestal stage illuminated in the center, the room empty but for one plush leather chair.

"What is the meaning of this place?" I asked.

"Some of us have access."

Money was the key to status and status was the key to power and power was the key to money and somewhere within this cycle there was meant to be an ending, a landing spot, a place of accomplishment where we say, yes, we have achieved what we came here to achieve. But instead, heart-pounding and out of breath, we beat on ever further, never realizing: Babygirl, we—are running circles.

Certain high-earning girls disappeared into VIP for hours. How could this be? How could one man pay hundreds, even thousands, for mere dances in a closet? There must be something else going on.

"Of course there's something else going on," Sheena laughed, shaking her head, gold hoops swinging in her ears, a Virginia Slim burning slow between her French-tipped nails.

For one thing, there were drugs going on.

There was one broad notorious for buying an eight ball of cocaine before each shift and eking that shit out all night in VIP. Incidentally, she was also an awful bitch, notorious for announcing that a tampon was too big for her exceptionally-tight pussy. The eight ball was an investment of a hundred or so bucks that would return perhaps even a thousand in revenue to this woman. There's a stereotype that strippers are all on drugs. In reality, it's the customers. And drugs, Miss Tight Pussy would provide. She kept her geeked-out clients glued to the couch for hours on end, alternately having the time of their lives and fiending like madmen, playing squeezy-time with her titties when not combing the carpet for spilled grains of blow, with each turn of the clock, another few hundred added to her earnings, another line tapped out on the table with the edge of his AmEx.

For another thing, there was sex going on.

Erotic indiscretions that have happened in VIP, any number of which I myself have been guilty, include but are not limited to: hand jobs, blow jobs, masturbation shows, girl-on-girl action, even intercourse. These activities are the natural deviances present in an establishment saturated in alcohol and sexuality, where behavioral boundaries proved oblique at every junction. Rules are not clearly posted at any location—what a buzzkill that would be!

"So the only difference between a floor dance and a VIP dance is the privacy?" I asked Sheena.

"Well. Officially."

"That's a hard sale."

"No shit."

"So what do you do? Straight lie to these dudes?"

"No. Don't lie. Lying is dangerous."

"Then how do I get them to sign off on hundreds if I tell them the truth? If I am honest?"

No, I can't technically kiss you, suck you, fuck you, put my pussy in your mouth. Now please come spend hundreds to not technically receive any of these bounties in a private room. However, let me insinuate—not with words but with glances and a hand under the table—that I am the kind of girl not wed to technicalities.

"Babygirl," Sheena replied, "I said nothing about being honest."

I was always ready to do some fucked-up shit.

By middle school, I determined that cigarette-smoking held the key to social success.

The cool kids were the bad kids, and the bad kids smoked. My chronic academic overachievement and compulsive poetry composition were no boon to the hardcore reputation I desired.

And so, while the other girls tried out for the junior cheerleading squad and learned NKOTB choreography, at the age of eleven I stood, resolute and alone, cigarette in one hand and a lighter in the other, before my bedroom mirror.

Obtaining the cigarette was easy. Hell, I'd obtained an entire pack, plucked from the open carton beneath the kitchen counter. I had my choice of brand, of course: Daddy's Marlboro 100s or Mama's Salem Slims. The choice was so clear that I didn't regard it as a choice at all: there were men's cigarettes, and there were women's. Women smoked menthol slims, the natural order of things, unseemly for a crass Cowboy Killer to be caught between her fingers. I didn't see a choice to be made: I stole from my mama. I see now, however, that I was always choosing—choosing to be a woman.

I prayed each night to be a woman. As my breasts pushed out in two swollen knots, as hair filled the space between my legs, in my diary I chronicled pleas for the final missing piece of my womanhood. "I am a woman in all ways," I wrote—"*except for one.*"

LeeAnne had her period. So did Amanda. Meredith got hers by the time she was in sixth grade. But mine?

Just wouldn't come.

At night, I'd beg God for blood.

However, if I couldn't force the Lord's timing on my blooming, I could damn sure learn to smoke.

Smoking was a very adult thing to do.

Also, rebellious.

One does not fully count as a smoker unless one is addicted, I surmised. And so, I set out to achieve that as well.

I will become the real thing no matter what it takes.

I placed the Salem between my lips.

I lit the match, held it smoldering to the cigarette's tip.

I sucked, ember sizzling. Smoke filled my mouth.

I hacked it out.

And then, I did it again.

You will learn this.

And not only that, but—

You will learn to want this. To need this. Your desire, growing bigger than your will, saying yes again and again to that which blatantly warns you, right there on the package, that it will kill you.

I welcomed this black fate.

Retching my way through each pull, that afternoon I taught myself how to smoke—until heaving, I surrendered, hand over mouth and toilet-bound.

On nights I'd perform poorly at the Styxx, coming home fists empty, I'd walk into my apartment a storm cloud. Bill would be waiting up with a peanut butter sandwich, a love offering, a sacrifice. In mere hours, he had to be at his own job. But he didn't care. He'd stay up late to see me.

It isn't often that a man will love you like that.

Don't squander it, like I did.

But squander it, I did.

My anger shut him down, his smile disappearing with the absence of my gratitude. I never yelled. I never talked ugly. I simply left the sandwich uneaten. I simply offered no thanks. I turned to mute stone.

I was angry. Angry when I came home broke. Angry at men for using my body for free. Since I was a child—used for free. I was mad, thinking on that redneck who drove me home from the lake when I was fifteen, fucked me in his rusty truck, fist clamped around my ponytail and pounding without so much as a kiss. Why did I let him do that? It wasn't a week after Daddy died before Joey was railing me as well, holding my arms above my head on a twin bed in his mama's basement. Wasn't a month after Joey beat my ass that he was fucking me again, this time on a ripped-out car seat in a basement where he was in hiding. Why did I do that? Why did I let them do that? I didn't know who I was angrier with—these men, or me.

"I wish you wouldn't strip," Bill admitted after months of closed-mouth acceptance, after the love-stoned newness that grants flaws immunity began to fade. When I'd put my wig on before leaving for work, he refused to admire me, his eyes darting from my beauty as if I were Medusa instead: fearsome and murderous, a head full of serpents and eyes that turn men into stone.

"This is when I look the best," I told him; "don't you think I'm pretty?"

"You don't look like *you* when you look like that."

I ached to love him with compassion. I yearned to act with consideration. But I could not love without annihilation. Wrap your arms around me and I become a detonation device. Hold on long enough and I will blow us both to smithereens. I could not forgive myself for who I was. Nor could I stop being that person.

I had been crowned the whore of Evilland before graduating high school—although who did the crowning, I'd never been able to pin down. Might've been me? I spent the year between high school and the Hot Styxx indulging in self-destructive behavior, sex with strangers, provocative outfits worn even for Sunday supper—I used my sexuality as a weapon and made it my identity, convinced this sword of sheer shirts and empty-eyed posing would wound my enemies, so addicted to its cold weight in my hand that I never knew when to put it down. Every time I used my body to manipulate the world into melding to my wishes, every time I did some low-down shit to get what I wanted, a tiny joyful voice inside me cheered: *fuck all y'all!*

But with Bill, it was different. Bill, I wanted to preserve in a glass jar. Sure, he'd be trapped in there. But at least I couldn't lose him.

And I could not, could *not* lose him.

I also could not act in such a way as to keep him.

He looked in my eyes, his own filling with tears.

"I love you so much," he said, "that it feels like pain."

The roof began to rattle with rain.

The sky lightened with the promise of dawn.

Bill's shift at Pizza Hut would start in only a few hours.

"Let's go for a walk," he suggested anyway.

"It's raining!"

"Better that way."

He wrapped his arm around my waist as we strode the wet streets of slumbering Richmond, holding tight to me, holding tight to our love, sensing the beginning of our end. Sensing my bitterness, my obsession with work, money, other men, and mostly, myself. Sensing my blindness to this goddamn angel offering himself at my feet while I ignored him.

As we walked, and I bitched, Bill would occasionally dip to the side of the road, plucking at people's gardens.

"Sheena made at least a grand tonight."

He visited flowerbeds.

"Me, on the other hand?"

He plucked a tulip.

"A hundred and eight dollars."

He stole a daisy.

"What does that say about me? One hundred and eight dollars?"

He bent again into a stranger's garden, his profile illuminated against the light of the street lamp.

And for a second, I saw him.

And for a second, I shut up.

I gazed upon this man, picking flowers in the night. This body to which I had drawn the map, every road memorized. This blonde hair. This Adam's apple, this collarbone, this bone-thin back with the tattoo in the center, those long hands, silver rings on his fingers, silver rings in his ears, a silver necklace around his neck—

He caught me admiring him, and strode over to me, grinning. He stuck his tongue at me and I burst out laughing, his kindness cracking my armor. What a great attitude on this man. He pulled me to him, his body pressing against my own, and kissed me so sweetly, so deliciously—dizzying, his tongue in my mouth.

Do you still want this, want us, his body asked mine, *even though you are sharp and angry and starving?* He pressed his mouth harder against my own, our need for one another growing even as the distance between our bodies closed. Here in this rainy street, we are one, and yet we are immeasurably apart, searching for one another in this embrace.

Yes, I want this—I cannot live without this—

He pulled his lips from mine and took a step back. From behind his back, he produced a bouquet.

He held the flowers out to me, so proud.

"What?" I gasped; "how—?"

Gardenias and tulips and magnolia blooms, daisies and weeds, all bundled together.

"I've been picking them this whole time, Lindsay. You didn't notice because you always keep your head down."

"Bit hot in here for that leather jacket, Handsome," Sheena teased, as together we approached my mark.

"Spent the day on my Harley," he answered, speaking to me instead of her.

"Oh," I said.

Sheena pinched my thigh.

I corrected myself.

"I'd love to see your Harley!"

"This is the girl I told you about," Sheena said, shuffling me closer towards his table.

"Name's Thomas." He reached out one great mitt to shake my hand.

"Why don't y'all get to know each other?" Sheena smiled, circling around to give Thomas a squeeze from behind, her great tits smashed against his back. Over his shoulder, she looked me in the eye. I sat down beside him.

"You know, Sheena and I were once an item," Thomas said as she walked away.

I was riding the tail end of childhood as I navigated my love for Bill. I was a brand-new woman at the daybreak of my adult life, one dawning under the shadow of the trauma that came before: swallowed sleeping pills and Daddy dead, cracked ribs and a court case, senior prom in bruises and Mama insane. I harbored no malice for those injured by the shrapnel of my existence. It was always an accident, and I always regretted it.

I was cheating on Bill, you see. Firstly, I was cheating on Bill with myself, or rather with that fishnet-wearing rock star whom I conjured every Tuesday, Friday, and Saturday, placing her desires above all else. Salving my wounds with an obsessive hustle, dollar amounts that proved that I was nobody's small town joke. Bill's wounds, I hadn't the capacity to consider. How my actions might affect him, I hadn't the scales to weigh.

And now, I was cheating on Bill with Thomas, too.

Just because I called it work didn't absolve my crimes.

Things were moving fast with Thomas, but then again, with the delusionally-psychotic, things often do. After Sheena introduced me to him that night, his visits to the Styxx became regular, constant. He'd sweep me off my feet and swing me in a circle by way of hello, squeeze me so hard that my rib, permanently unstable from the beating, would slide out of place, a sickening slip of bone against slippery insides. He'd take me to his table and set me in his lap, his arms wrapped across my body, an announcement to all passers-by that I belonged to him. He squeezed me even tighter when Sheena circled the floor.

I could tell right away that Thomas won't right in the head. This knowledge, I decided to mobilize to my advantage. I was opportunistic. Ambitious. Hungry. I didn't question my cultivation of his madness, nor the danger of getting too close.

"I have a purple heart," he claimed, early into our relationship.

"George Bush has a conspiracy against me," he told me, a few weeks later.

"I could put you into my will," he suggested, by the end of the month.

He arrived to the club with a sheet of yellow legal paper scribbled in the handwriting of a lunatic, listing the assets he promised to bequeath me: two horses on a farm in Delaware. A home in Mechanicsville. A collection of seventeen golden bars. A purple heart. His Harley.

His Harley was the only thing I knew actually existed, because I saw it parked outside the Styxx every night the Lord sent.

"Should I die," he said, handing me his handwritten will, moist with sweat, "I want you to have all of this."

"Alternately," he added, "you could simply marry me and I wouldn't have to die."

His grandiose fantasies were already in place when I arrived into his life; he needed only a paper doll to paste into the scene. A wife to install into the nice home he imagined he possessed—Sunday lunch, pot roast, and then we'd put it in the wind for Delaware, go ride the horses. Thomas was a Desert Storm vet with PTSD, a traumatic brain injury, and an addiction to masculinity fueled by insecurity and funded by a regular check from Uncle Sam sent as an apology. He took that money to the Cherokee casino in North Carolina in the daytimes and brought his winnings to me at night, his manhood affirmed by the thickness of his wallet and my plump young body on his lap.

"I dreamed I was in the latrine last night," he confessed, "and I woke up pissing in my closet."

With that, I led him into the back.

I'd listen intently as he shared his stories of war. He wanted nothing more than a Salisbury steak and mashed potatoes in that desert, he told me. There had been a woman back home, but she'd stopped writing. He'd seen a man's leg fly through the air, blood spraying a rainbow of life and death all at once.

The other soldiers called him a fag because he cried sometimes, and one night, Thomas awoke to the butt of a rifle slapped flat across his stomach. The dark room filled with the laughter of his comrades as Thomas choked for air.

Thomas didn't want sex from me. Honestly, the soldiers could have been right about his sexual predilections. What Thomas wanted was love. But the only way to get love in this club was to pay for sex, or something close to it.

"There's something wrong with Thomas," I told Sheena, a few weeks into my relationship with him. "He has conspiracy theories about the president. He claims to own golden bars. He's talking about putting me into his will."

"Oh," she answered, filing her nails. "He's gotten to the will."

"How do you know about the will?"

She looked up, her file frozen in place.

"Did you know he was insane when you introduced us?"

She looked back down, file flying.

There are lines you draw in the beginning, things you said you would never do.

As my ability to metabolize Thomas's emotions grew, my relationship with him accelerated. As our relationship accelerated, my earnings—and his delusions—grew. To keep the money coming, I needed only serve his false gods with my smile, my affection, and occasionally, some friction.

He took my chin into his hand in that dark VIP room, pulled my face inches from his own. "Lux, I want to take you out of here. We can live a good life."

"Sure," I stuttered, then rode him into silence.

I'd rather grind than listen to him spew.

He closed his eyes, turned me around backwards.

One night, at the close of a lengthy evening with him, I filled in the tip-out sheet and noticed with a start:

My god. I've earned more than every other woman here.

Including Sheena.

"Nobody pays this much for conversation," Bill said later when, giggling, I counted my money on the bedroom floor. He turned his back to me that night, disappearing into sleep as if he weren't in my bed at all.

When the love runs out, it leaves quiet, piece by piece, in the small things—the silence between your bodies, the way he doesn't show up in the middle of the day. When the love goes, it leaves in secret, until one day you reach into your pocket expecting a bounty, but your hand comes up empty, where once it was full.

Bill's nights at my apartment were waning, his patience for my mood swings in decline. I could tell I was losing him, and I was frantic, a woman drowning, beating at the surface for something to hold to, the sea slipping through my hands.

The same tricks that I used to hypnotize customers, I used in an attempt to win back his affections: say his name. Let my mouth hang open. Be interested, not interesting. I am a vessel to receive you.

A mistake, to believe a snake charmer can fool him who is not a snake.

"Let me meet your mother," I begged, a final bid to insinuate myself more deeply into his life.

There was no one in the world Bill loved more than his mother.

I hated her for that.

She suspected the same of me, and hated me in return.

I had only to walk into her apartment for her to catch on to my machinations.

54

We women can detect one another's tricks.

Bill's mother had been hit with the bad end of his parents' marriage. He felt that she had been treated mean. Her vulnerability fed his tenderness for her, the way we love the runt of a litter, the way we love a three-legged dog, the way we love the wounded, the way we loved each other.

She wouldn't look at me when we entered her home, as jealous of me as I was of her. She could recognize my power, feel it working on her son. The way I held his hand through our entire visit—Jesus! Possessive. Hungry. She didn't have to tell me: I made her sick. I walked into her door, sat on her couch for two hours, and then walked back out without her so much as giving me a glance. She didn't greet me when I entered. She ignored my questions. Didn't offer me a cigarette when she offered Bill one.

The girl with the dark eyes and the dark hair had a pull so strong that even she could recognize it, working on her son. "She's too much," I imagined her whispering to him when I wasn't around.

Too much. Too much need. Too much pain. Too much baggage. Too much control. I was demanding. Bossy. Afraid. Hold on tight, little girl, or he will slip away. Just like Daddy. Just like every boy who never loved me no matter how many pounds of flesh I paid. I am too much of everything, and everyone leaves.

"I don't think she likes me," I said to Bill, as we drove away.

I wanted him to comfort me, to tell me I was wrong. Instead he said nothing, his mind working in silence, walled off against me.

I called Mama.

"She hated me!"

"What in the world could she hate you for?"

"She's jealous!"

"Well, you know how women can be with their sons."

Mama, of course, bitterly despised every woman either of my brothers had ever loved.

"But I need her to like me, Mama."

"Why?"

"Because I need *him* to love me."

"Oh, no. You're not starting this shit."

"You don't understand—"

"*I* don't understand? I had a whole big life before you. You beg a man for love, and you'll end up cutting down every tree in your yard."

Here, of course, Mama was referring to the Great Landscaping Shame of Cousin Jess.

Cousin Jess was Great Aunt Mattie's daughter. One of us.

Jess was a married woman, but her husband was gone a lot.

Yet Jess was still young and pretty.

And so, she wasn't satisfied to live in some man's absence.

Jess was young and pretty—

And always cold.

Her yard was dark, you see. Made the whole house chilly.

Throughout her lawn grew large trees, oaks and pines and magnolias casting shadows, leaving the home beneath them perpetually cool.

Shivering in a bathrobe one morning, Jess looked through her window, and wished for sun.

A blanket of sun.

And so, Jess called the local landscaper.

"I need you to let in some light," she told him over the phone. She had never felt so bold, dialing that man's number, asking for what she wanted without a lick of permission.

He arrived the next day, strong and shining, a mane of mahogany hair piled into a bun on his head, every curve of his chest, hugged by a thin white tee. She met him at the door, braless in a wife beater.

Lord Jesus, she was taking it to new levels.

"That one," she said, pointing to the biggest tree in the yard. "Cut it down."

"Are you sure?" he asked, his eyes gliding over her breasts. "There's nothing wrong with that tree."

"I'm sure."

"And it could take me days to finish the job."

She nodded.

Anything. Anything to be on fire. Anything to wake in the morning, heart racing, not with dread of another day flat with dishes and laundry and loneliness and regret, but instead with elation, expectancy, hunger. The landscaper will arrive in two hours, meaning two hours to prepare her body with razors and lotions and blush and perfume to appear as if she had done nothing to prepare at all. Two hours within which she can masturbate on a balled-up towel pressed against the corner of the bathroom counter, coming in silence, shuddering without sound, alone and quiet in her pleasure as she had trained herself to be. No. This is not her life. This moment—now—this man's eyes on her—*this* is her life. She doesn't know this man, doesn't know his name. She might not ever ask. Nonetheless, she wants him. Wants him to consume her. To obliterate her. To turn her into dust, howling. When he arrives at her door on the third day, chainsaw in hand, she hooks her fingers into his belt loops and pulls his body against hers. *Make love to me*, she prays, but she can't say it. He squeezes her waist with his two strong hands, chuckles, pushes her off him. This is a mercy. He is a light illuminating the exact way she shouldn't go. I wonder how many other starving women in tank tops this landscaper has bewitched?

In two days, he destroyed the first tree.

It would take weeks to destroy them all.

"Are you sure?" he asked, each time. "The only thing wrong with these trees is that you keep cutting them down."

She *was* sure. As magnolias crashed and the sky opened up, for the first time in a long time, Jess didn't feel cold. Indeed, she awoke sweating in the night. As the landscaper ran out of plants to decimate, Jess searched the barren landscape for another sacrifice, another day worth wearing a wife beater, another day she wasn't locked inside and invisible and dead, another day of his tight T-shirt and hungry eyes.

Until finally—there really was nothing left. Not a tree in the yard. Not a single bush. Not a weed to pull. Her home, which had once been blanketed by shade, sat now upon a scorching plot of dirt.

"Well, I guess she liked it that way," I told Mama, when she finished the story. "Empty."

"It don't matter if she liked it that way!" Mama replied. "She fucked up her whole yard!"

CHAPTER FIVE

THAT STUFF'S IN THE PAST

Thomas liked me face down, ass up. He slid a hand across a cheek and squeezed while I straddled him backwards. His roving touch made me nervous, but I allowed it. If we got caught, it was my job on the line, not his. My compliance kept the money coming—yet my compliance also threatened my job. A hand caught in the wrong place would get a bitch jerked up quick.

I was trained in this watchful, fearful catering to the desires of men. They'd never get in trouble for the things we'd do together. Crimes committed in allegiance with men were punishable only for women. However, on the other side of these risks, potential rewards awaited. And so, I took the risks. Many of us women did. It used to be love I was gambling for, giving head while watching my bedroom door. Now the reward was different, though the chips remained the same. Throw several pounds of flesh onto the table, and if I am lucky, I will win. Win what, I never knew. Money, sure, there was that. But there was more to it than that.

Thomas tugged at my thong, sliding the tip of his finger beneath the thin band of spandex.

Two things—

One: if I allowed him this access, I could prevent him from telling me stories about the blood of boys watering the sands of Arabia, a girl's photo found in the wreckage left by a hidden landmine, her sweet smile still wearing braces, this photo the only thing intact in the shredded jacket of a shredded man; a single stray kitten that survived the whole shebang, one ear torn off but still mewing. When Thomas started talking about those things, he started talking fast, and although my job was to smile, I was scared of men who talked fast.

Two: my body was reacting—to this friction, to this man whom I found frightening at best and revolting at worst, and yet I felt pleasure, and yes, I *sought* pleasure in this perverse concoction.

Nothing would please Thomas more than to know my body had joined this ride, was quickening pace now according to my own sensation, the attentions of my tempo stolen from him and given to my own desire. He grabbed my hips, trying to move me faster against his lap. I held firm in my rhythm. I'd faked many orgasms for him over these months together, sighing his name with a tremble. Yet as exquisitely the waves swelled, gathered, pounded, I controlled my quake, issued no moan. This pleasure was mine alone, and I wouldn't share it.

When death visits your home, everyone else leaves. Friends send flowers and casseroles but not their bodies, their presence, their words. *NO ONE WANTS YOU*, I scrawled in Sharpie across the wall of my bedroom closet, in the days of my daddy's dying. It was not an untruth.

It was at this point in my life that I met Joey. He was four years older than me, twenty-one to my seventeen.

I was eating Ecstasy in a trailer park when we first locked eyes. He caught me dancing on a table and like many of the boys there, liked what he saw.

He, however, was not a boy.

He—was a man.

A few days after Daddy's funeral, Joey took me out to lunch and put gas in my car.

"My dad is dead, too, you know," he told me.

That was all I ever wanted from him.

Not the sandwich. Not the gas.

Not the big bad thing that was coming to serve as the great ghastly distorter of my upcoming womanhood.

No. I wanted the dead dad.

Together, we were two half-orphans. I loved that about us. I was a kid living at home with my newly-widowed mother, to whom I was as unnoticeable as a moth in our newly shared darkness. The few friends I did have, kids my age, stopped inviting me to Bubba's for milkshakes or Twin Arches for weed circles. A dead parent is a horrifying, unmentionable thing. Do you imagine he is rotting yet? Do worms eat his eyes? Do you think I will ever again feel his rough palm, the hand of a working man? Only in dreams, right? Only in dreams, because just like Daddy, God is dead, too. Let's change the subject.

"What was your father's name?" Joey asked, half an Italian sub in one hand and my deepest yearnings in the other.

"David," I answered. "David Burton."

"David Burton."

"But his friends called him Kool."

"My father's name was Giuseppe. Like me."

"Tell me about him."

"You first," he said.

And thus, the affair began.

Daddy's body wasn't even cold.

Six months later, Joey would brutalize me with enough black-eyed fury to bruise my brain, but before that, he filled up my every hole with a darkness I devoured like a woman guzzling venom, thirsting to death for death.

Bill wasn't stupid. When flowers arrived at my apartment addressed to "Lux," he decided that was the extent of what he would accept, and he stormed out and didn't return all day. When he did come back to me, it was after midnight, and we were both drunk and furious.

"I went to a party," he slurred.

Party? He went to a party without me?

"You live a whole fucking *life* without me," he answered.

You can't do this, and you can't do that, I began, listing the catalogue of rules he had broken. Yet frankly, my dear, he didn't give a damn. You could see it in his eyes. No pain. Instead, amusement. His eyes laughed at my demands—demands I had no right to make.

And so, I slapped him.

Full in his face, as hard as I could.

That delicate face, too pretty for a man. Soft lips. High cheekbones. Eyes of blue. Not a mark, a line, a wrinkle to be seen; still a child; we both were.

Now, twenty years later, I have a friend, a woman with a past. But she found a man to love her anyway. "Do you know what he says to me," she tells me, when she describes their love. "He says to me, *I love you all the way back*."

All the way back. Even into the grisly horrors that marked the path between then and now. The ugly things we've done, the ghouls we hide. All the way back I love you, along every twisted turn and stumble that brought you to me.

That face, those eyes that had gazed upon me so tenderly, forehead pressed against mine as our bodies rocked in unison; that face, with one crooked tooth that caught his lip when he smiled; that face, who'd smiled upon me sweetly when I'd never tasted sweetness a day in my life—

That was the face I slapped.

That man of blue eye and soft lip and lovemaking on the floor—

now wore my handprint across his cheek.

He had loved me all the way back.

And here I was, shitting all over it.

They say violence breeds violence, so maybe that's why I hit Bill. Maybe that's why I would eventually let other men pay to abuse me. My mama, she was hit, too. Granny as well. Come to think of it, Great Granny as well. Come to think of it, all us women in the family. Getting your ass kicked was a rite of passage into womanhood, just as sure as starting your period.

The night Joey beat me began as a good time. A local drug dealer in Danville had around a hundred people crammed into his wrong-side-of-the-tracks shack that night, and where I come from, that's one hell of a party. When I walked my nubile teenage body into that Evilland shithole filled with twenty-something men guzzling forties, it's fair to say, heads turned. I was young, and wounded, the easiest shot in the forest.

Joey bought us some acid, which we promptly ate. He then began pounding beers. The man was a marvel with the drinking—unparalleled. Within the first hour, he drank twenty-four beers.

And that is how Joey accomplished the unheard-of feat of out-drinking an acid trip.

Fellow revelers gathered to witness this anomaly—a man so drunk that he put LSD to sleep. Everyone was laughing at this wild man passed out cold on the couch, but—

I knew there was going to be a problem.

Alcohol always made Joey enraged.

Over the course of our relationship, when drunk, Joey had committed the following:

1. Choked me in a rainy parking lot
2. Broken a cop's hand during a scuffle
3. Attempted to rip the transmission out of my car
4. Lit on fire every photo of himself and his father
5. Lit on fire every photo of himself as a child

Vomit spilled from his mouth like a mudslide upon the upholstery. A guy at the party stuck French fries up his nose. Someone drew a dick on the back of his neck. I turned him over on his side and laid his spewing head in my lap so he wouldn't die.

But when he woke up, all he wanted to do was kill me.

He said I'd sucked every dick at the party while he was asleep.

"Asleep," he called it.

Eyes empty, he leapt to his feet and pointed at me.

"Fucking whore."

I ran downstairs and out of the door.

He followed me into the street, taking a pit stop to piss in the front yard. He didn't even turn his back, dick dangling for all to see.

"I'll get him out of here," I promised the other guests, as I searched the street for my car, struggling to locate reality within this acid trip.

With explosive ferocity, Joey rammed me from behind, pushing me off the sidewalk. I fell to my knees in the street.

A friend of mine from childhood—an older boy named Scott—ran over to me, took my chin in his hand. "*Do not go home with him,*" he commanded.

I put Joey in my car anyway.

And that's when, with a gurgling snort, Joey spit in my face. Thick spit, ribboned with snot and jeweled with bubbles, tangled in my eyelash, dripped from my nose.

"He spit in my face! He spit in my fucking face!" I hollered, falling out of the car.

At this, Scott came running.

He yanked Joey from the vehicle by his armpit, stood him square on his feet, and reared back. I covered my eyes.

I'd never heard the sound of bone on bone before. Like a gunshot, or lightning: a sharp, standing-alone sound, a crack that splits the night in two. When I uncovered my eyes, there was my old friend, illuminated in the darkness by a flickering street lamp, cradling his shattered fist. Beneath his feet, Joey lay face-down on the asphalt, blood pooling around his head.

"You killed him," I whispered.

But he hadn't.

I called Bill a dozen times after our fight. Finally, he picked up. Finally, he agreed to come over. We made love that night with crazed voraciousness. We were desperate for each other, but this time it was different. This time, we knew—this is the last of the drugs, and we are out of money. When he came, he cried out in pleasure, and then in pain. Afterwards, he sat silent and dark on the side of my bed, head in his hands. I knew then that he would never make love to me again.

Nothing stings like a Last Time. My heart was pierced with this cruel certainty.

Our love was a ripe peach, fuzzy on the outside, soft to touch, sweet to taste. And yet my fingers had dug too deeply, destroying the fruit until only the pit remained, a stone slippery with nectar to remind me that once, sweetness had lived here, juice streaming down my chin.

"I'm done," he said. "Just...done."

I sunk to my knees on the floor, laid my head in his lap, and begged him: *please don't leave.* "You'll never forget me," I promised him, a curse and a wish. "You'll be thinking about me in twenty years!"

"I know that," he said, then made his way to my door.

"Your mother never liked me!" I spat as he descended my fire escape.

He paused on the stairs, looked up at me. In his eyes I saw all his pain collected, neat and tidy, contained and not exploding like mine.

"No. She didn't like you."

"Well, what does she know?" I hollered after his car as he drove away. "She can't keep a man either!"

Joey stood up and smiled as if he wasn't just felled like a tree. Blood poured from his mouth, gore streaming down his chin, soaking the street with his blood. Half of one of his front teeth was broken on a diagonal. A sharp tooth now. A shark's tooth now.

When Scott went inside to ice his hand, I used the chance to escape with Joey.

Since Daddy had died and Joey had stepped in, my life had become his absolutely. No person, no crime, no snot spat in my face, could stop me from clinging to this anchor taking me to the bottom of the ocean.

When we got out of the car at his mother's house, he kicked me square in the ass, sending me to the ground, knocking the breath out of me. With a great leap he stomped on my thigh. I carried his shoe print on my leg all the way until prom.

I ran into his house and into the back bedroom, locked the door behind me, curled up on the bed, and started praying.

Dear Jesus, prom is only two weeks away—

Possessing the unsurpassable strength of the psychotically enraged, Joey tore through the door, the lock popping as easy as a gumball out of a machine. With slow, deliberate steps, he bared his broken teeth at me and growled.

I looked into his eyes, sending my love through my own. *See me. Remember me, your darling half-orphan, your broken girl—*

But he—wasn't there. His eyes were black orbs.

In an instant he was on me, cracking my ribs as I covered my face.

In another instant, he had me by the hair, slamming my head into the wall.

Searing light. Spots swimming behind my eyelids. The sound of the ocean, peaceful, sweet. How easy it is to die.

The commotion woke his mama and she rushed in to investigate. He raised his arm stiff like an oar and swung his cupped hand against her ear. A thin line of blood crept down her neck. I'd expected horror in her face. Instead, I saw only disappointment. And I knew in that moment—this isn't the first time this has happened.

Joey's twelve-year-old brother was having a sleep-over that night. He called the police from his bedroom. This wasn't a first for him, either, the sound of fists on women.

After the police restrained Joey and put him in the car, one of the sleepover boys sat beside me at the kitchen table and slipped a cigarette into my hand. "I stole this from my dad," the boy whispered as he sidled up beside me, placing in my hand his one single indulgence, his squirrelled away treasure, a solitary Marlboro Red. "I've been saving it for the best time."

For his crimes against me, Joey would be sentenced to six weeks in jail.

Turns out, you can beat up your mother and teenage girlfriend and not get into much trouble.

Like Joey would tell me, a lifetime later:

"That stuff's in the past."

Joey's dad didn't just die. He killed himself. Joey's mother found him slumped in the car in their garage. Joey was just a boy then.

"That stuff's in the past."

A dark spot in my soul wants men to hit me. Hurt me. My head fills with a midnight ocean and I'm happy to drown. I've stopped trying to cure this. Yet still, I flinch at innocent movements. Yet still, I have nightmares.

"That stuff's in the past."

I snuck around and fucked Joey after he beat me up, while he was in hiding from my brothers who were trading pot to losers for clues.

I have hit men, good men, men who didn't deserve it.

Two half-orphans, alone together. Two half-orphans, breaking the numbness with violence to the point that breaking is feeling, and so it is welcome. Two-half orphans, the stronger one paying the weaker one the father's tab of abandonment and alienation. I don't know any more who was who.

That stuff's in the past.
Never.

CHAPTER SIX
My Name is Lindsay

Gone.

Gone were the arms around my waist, the crooked eyetooth, the openness that opened me. Gone were the silver-ringed fingers running slow across my body, the only hands ever to touch me soft. Gone were the afternoon deliveries, love on the floor. Gone.

And could you blame him?

Everyone, stay away. Honestly, no one touch me. I bring destruction, complete and contagious. The disease of my existence infects all who come close. I will now evaporate into atoms and dissipate into the night sky, back to black from whence I come.

I laid on the couch for nine days straight after Bill left me, balling up pieces of bread and sliding them down my throat when the gnaw of hunger became too strong. I replaced meals with cigarettes and water with wine and sleep with self-flagellation. All the things I'd done wrong, my god, let me count the ways. This could take a while. This could take nine days.

On day ten without him, I arose from the couch, determined to drive by his house. I wouldn't approach him, no, wouldn't knock on the door. I would only check his bedroom window, hope for a shaft of light, proof that he still lived and breathed. I was obsessed. Cursed. Sick.

But first, I had a few things to pick up.

At the 7-11, I placed a Mountain Dew on the counter along with five packs of Unisom.

"Ma'am, we cannot sell you all of that."

"I'll put the drink back."

"No. The pills. We cannot sell you that volume of pills."

"How many can you sell me?"

"One pack at a time, ma'am."

I ate one, two, three pills on my way to Bill's.

I turned into his neighborhood, turned down his street. Drove slowly by his house. Indeed, his bedroom window shone bright into the night. He was home.

Wait—

There is movement—

Is that his silhouette behind the blinds?

Does he, too, stare into the night for me?

Yes!

He stands in the window even now!

Bill, is your refusal of my love, your refusal to answer my phone calls, an armor you must wear lest I crush you with my unending need and uncontrollable trauma? Do you don that armor reluctantly? As you steel yourself against the ringing phone, as you drive past my apartment without stopping by, do you chant oaths and incantations to protect yourself from me? I'd been loved. My god, I had been loved. Bill, you gave that to me. I've lived a whole life since then. I've been with many other men. Yet I've been unable to forget the way you looked at me on that rainy street in Richmond, Virginia, flowers behind your back. Do you stand by that window now, my love, peering through the blinds to spy my car, to see me behind the wheel consuming sleeping pills and

Mountain Dew? I am trying to die. But I cannot die. My heart beats on at the mere bidding of your profile.

And then—the window turned dark.

And he—was gone again.

I drove home, stumbled to the couch, passed out for seventeen hours, then laid off work for another week.

Of course, no amount of drowning depression can break the addiction or forestall rent.

Lashes glued, makeup applied, smile plastered: back at it.

When stalking the strip club floor, your real life falls into the shadows.

Drink, bitch, drink. Numb it all.

I laid my spinning head down on the dressing room counter.

"For fuck's sake, kid, pull it together," Sheena spat. "Do you know how much pain there is in this world? Get used to pain. Life is *made* of pain."

She shoved me with a bump of her hip.

"Get up. It's time to work."

I raised my head, blinked my eyes.

"Where's Thomas?" Sheena asked. "Shouldn't you be with him?"

"I haven't seen Thomas since me and my boyfriend broke up…"

"You mean all this time you've been laying off work, you haven't reached out to Thomas? Not once? Not even a phone call?"

"Should I have?"

"Wow," Sheena said. "You're stupider than I thought."

Everyone loved us when we were on—the customers, management—hell, even the other girls. Sheena, six-foot-three in those heels, delivering punchlines bar-side, sprinkling compliments with the grace of a royal. Me, the wide-eyed colt, faking naivety, amazed at everything. Men like a little bit of both, you see—the guide, and the idiot. A woman to lead them where they are afraid to go, and a girl stupid enough to be led.

"You know why I like you?" Sheena asked me, as the DJ called her to the stage.

"I've always wondered."

"Because you remind me of myself. Ten years ago. Young, dumb, and killing it."

She stumped out her cigarette and stood to approach the stage.

"And that's also why I hate you."

I marveled alongside the tip rail as Sheena spun, one hand on the pole and the other pinching daintily the corner of her satin robe, pirouetting like a white-trash Cinderella. She looked at me and in her eyes I saw the ghosts of the women who came before us, loose women in bawdy shows, high school whores from the wrong area codes, girls with daddy issues and crazy mamas: women like me. I held court stage-side for the entirety of her set, spellbound, drunk. Gaze upon the glory to which this woman has ascended! What life had been like for her, I did not know. I did imagine, however. In the shape of her body, I spun a story that sounded like my own. She didn't come from much. Was not ever expected to be much. Looked over. Teased. Reviled. All the pain had been an investment—all of it, worth it. Just look at her now, a golden-maned giant, collecting her return. In Sheena, I saw everything I could become. Onto her body, I wrote the story of myself.

"If you think you're taking my place around here," she said as she dismounted the stage, "you're fucking crazy."

"Where have you been?" he asked, eyes bright and searching. Thomas's gaze travelled my body as if he could discern the answer to my absence on my skin.

"He's been coming in every day looking for you," the waitress whispered when she brought us our drinks.

"Have you been sick," he asked, his hands squeezing my arms, my shoulders, running through my hair, testing the reality of my physical body. "It's really you," he muttered, as if I have died rather than missed a couple weeks of work.

"Follow me," he said, and led me to VIP. "I've got something that will make you feel better."

Once alone in that dark closet, he opened an envelope filled with a stack of official-looking documents.

"I want to put your name on these," he said.

I scanned the papers in his lap. Loan agreements? Titles?

"I want to take you out of this life, and I've got the plans to do it, too. We'll get married soon. We have to move quick, though, because there's a conspiracy against me, starting right up top with the president of the United States." He shoved a hundred dollar bill, balled up and sweaty, into my hand. "Here's a tip," he muttered. "We need to hit the road tonight—George Bush Senior and Junior *both* could be coming for me at any time, might be now, might be tomorrow—"

"Thomas—"

"Might be next week, or the week after that..."

"Are you...okay...?"

"Hush and goddamn do as I say!"

I backed away.

Thomas ran his finger along the indentation in his skull. "It's this, isn't it? *It's this, isn't it?*" He slapped his head.

I took him, trembling, into my arms.

"Go home, baby," I whispered. "Get ready for our escape." I clasped his hands into my own, holding them until his broad palms fluttered into stillness, like the slow stuttering beat of the wings of a moth.

The curtain parted, and the bouncer stuck his head into the door.

"Everything okay?"

"Just fine!" I replied.

"What's it like to have a regular?" I had asked Sheena, months ago, when this all began.

"Some things are better to learn for yourself," she had told me, then.

Well, I'd learned for myself.

"He's delusional," I told Sheena, when I found her in the dressing room. "Psychotic."

"How 'bout it."

"You knew this?"

She shrugged.

"So why did you set me up with him, then? If you knew he was crazy?"

"You got kids, Babygirl? No. Of course you don't."

"What do your children have to do with this?"

"Thomas writes you letters, doesn't he? Gives you his will, property titles? Sends you flowers, maybe even to your home? Do you have a husband, Lux; do you have babies? No, you don't. Well, let me tell you what I had. I *had* a husband. I *had* babies. And let me tell you how much husbands and babies appreciate Mama riding dick for roses."

I heard him before I saw him, speeding beneath the street lamps, perched upon his Harley.

"Lux," he hollered, "Lux!"

Keep your eyes on the road. Pretend you do not hear him.

Bile burned the back of my throat.

The lights of nighttime Richmond sped across my windshield.

How could I have known he would lie in wait behind the old tobacco plant across from the club? How could I have known he would surveil the parking lot, wait for me to exit, follow my car for a mile or more before I even knew he was there at all?

I turned left—he turned left.

I turned right—he turned right.

I made circles around the block—he made circles around the block.

"Lux!" he yelled at the corner of Broad and Roseneath.

"Lux!" he bellowed from Lombardy.

"Lux!" he called across these streets, my neighborhood, my home.

My god, what fury had I wrought? What dangerous game had I played? I'd seen dancers collecting gifts—heard tell of others collecting cars, even houses, from men. I'd never been so naïve to think these treasures came without some exchange. "There ain't no such thing as a free lunch," my daddy always said, growing up. I never knew what he meant before. But I did now.

Thomas screamed for me in the night. He yearned for me to notice him, take him into my arms, consume his agony, feast upon his horror, and spit out diamonds in return. He threw into the air a word he'd come to associate with my being, my body, my smile, my silence. Yet what he had known of me— had always been an illusion.

"Lux," he yelled, "Lux," but he never knew:

My name is Lindsay.

The next morning, I called Mama.

"I need to come home for a bit," I told her.

"I figured eventually you would."

I was not eager to return to Danville. But I knew I could not survive myself without distraction. I knew the hooligans of Evilland; could find the right pills from the wrong people; could fuck some random rednecks to get my mind off things. Could smoke cigarettes on Mama's porch a hundred or more miles from Bill's dark window. Could escape the shadows of my losses.

Mama hated that I smoked cigarettes. I smoked them anyway. Ever since her heart attack, Mama had put down the Salems. "Although," she has since admitted, "if they made 'em so that they wouldn't kill you, I'd buy a hundred packs today."

"Wish you would quit that shit," she said, as I lit my second one off the first.

"Says the woman who made me a smoking fetus."

Mama tried to snatch the cigarette from my mouth.

"Back off," I said.

"That shit will kill you."

"I don't care."

"I want to know why Bill left you."

Mama was nosy. Always had been. She had read every word of every diary I ever wrote. So it was no surprise that she'd been rifling through my suitcase since I'd arrived home. No surprise that she found among my items a rubber-banded stack of ones. A matchbox reading "Club Hot Styxx." A hot pink thong.

She took a step forward, approaching me, her lips folding into a thin line.

"Are you—a stripper?"

In a previous life, I might've lied.

But now, mired in misery with nothing to lose, I had become spiteful. Mean.

"Yep, sure am," I answered, with all the glibness of a bitchy teen.

"So that's why he left you."

I glared at her.

"And he was a good man, too."

I focused on the burning tip of my cigarette.

"How could you demean yourself like this?"

I looked up. Fed up. Not again. Not another litany of reasons why I was awful. Not another checklist of blame. I get it, Mama, I get it.

"Demean myself?" I replied, flicking my cigarette into her yard. "Stripping is the best thing to ever happen to me!"

"Who do you think you're fooling," she asked, "you or me? Because it sure as shit ain't me."

CHAPTER SEVEN
In the Blood

Mama was playing piano the night we released Fred into the wild. She'd purchased the instrument for me, but in the absence of my dedication, Mama had taken over. Each night she practiced Chopin as if she hadn't grown up in a home where folks spoke in terms such as "yonder" and "fixin' to."

As a sonata filled the air, somewhere in that great magnolia a squirrel's ears perked up. Growing from a blind-eyed infant into a full-grown adult to the tune of this nightly piano practice, perhaps Fred had developed an affinity for the sound of Chopin. Maybe he'd learned to rely on its comforting regularity, a musical harmony that announces: a family lives here; this is a home. Maybe he longed to be nestled beneath a human chin, his belly rubbed.

Regardless of the cause, on the second night after we set Fred free, Mama played piano, and a banging began on our door.

From my spot next to my window, I heard something—first, a dull thud.

Then another.

Then another, louder this time.

I sped toward the sound.

By the time I made it downstairs, Daddy was already there, squirrel in his hand, lunch box at his feet.

"He was throwing himself at the door," Daddy said. "Throwing his whole body against that damn door."

"Can he stay this time?"

Mama stood from her seat at the piano bench and looked to Daddy, this man of such masculine hardness, now nose to nose with a squirrel, both of them thrilled to meet once again.

"Well, shit," Mama said. "Bring him back in."

I remained in Danville over summer break, palling around with a gang of boys who shared everything, me included. They traded shifts at the Texaco station on the edge of town, out toward Twin Arches. Drive out that way, and storefronts give way to wilderness. You're in the country now.

Among the Texaco boys, I had my favorite.

"Can't turn the lights on or somebody might see us," he whispered, his body moving against mine in the darkness of the garage. He was a skateboarding king and the handsomest of them all. He laced his fingers into mine, breath hot on my throat. A temporary elixir. A fix for now.

Hurt.

Who was I hurting for?

Bill.

Beneath him, Joey.

Beneath him, Daddy.

Beneath all of them: me.

A child, at the onset of this shit. This begging. This neediness. My very first diary entries, waxing obsessively about boys while deliberating over what Santa would bring. When I was five years old, a classmate named Daniel kissed me under a tree. I thought about that kiss for the rest of my life. Where did this obsession come from? Pitiful. Pathetic. Was it congenital? Clearly it was illness. Weakness. A shame. Maybe I couldn't blame it on anyone. Maybe it was in the blood. Maybe—I couldn't even blame me.

I fell in lust with the skateboarder that summer; it was easy to do. Shirtless, tan, body carved with compact strength and just the right amount of dirt, he sailed his skateboard across the auto pit in the garage, a joint behind his ear. Irresistible.

Not only was he irresistible.

He was also a Jesus freak.

Sometimes, between kisses, beyond the shadows in the auto garage, somewhere in the light of day underneath a tree in Grove Park, he would express his remorse: guilt over his weed-smoking, drinking, partying—but mostly, guilt over me.

"God wants something different for us," he said, eyes misting as he gazed into the distance.

"God's not real."

"See what I mean, Lindsay?"

After two weeks of dry-humping and hand jobs, he finally relinquished his virginity to me on a picnic table in the dark. After that, he wasn't interested anymore. I had become a stumbling block on his path of righteousness—a role I had become accustomed to playing.

I had meant to wield my body like a sword, turn my seduction of men into revenge: this time, they would be the ones wanting, and begging, and needing! Yet their need only lasted so long. So short, their need, dissolved with the first thrust. Instead of powerful, I felt embarrassed. Poisonous. Something another man didn't want.

One night, as I begged his attention with sad eyes and grasping hands, he looked me in the face and gave it to me straight.

"I will never be in love with you, Lindsay."

I couldn't imagine, then, how he could be so decisive. How were men so sure in their rejections? Wasn't there a way to change their minds?

Again, the lesson was presented, but not for the last time: there is no begging love. Love doesn't care what you want.

A few weeks after returning to Richmond for the Fall semester, I ran into Bill at the late-night pizza joint. I had another quick fix in tow, a dude five inches shorter and three years younger than me, a kid enamored with the glamour of my darkness, a band-aid for a bullet hole.

There would never be another Bill.

Some kind of love only happens once—that's what makes it precious. That's what turns a kiss in a hallway into a jewel that you fondle in your pocket over the rest of your life, something to inspect later, when love is over, and you feel dead.

"Aren't you going to say hello to Bill?"

Quick Fix pointed at the counter, where there stood the greatest love of my young life ordering a pepperoni. "Well, aren't you?" he teased again, and he meant it as a joke, but I didn't take it as one.

Nothing could have kept me from Bill.

And so, I strode up to that counter. Sidled up by Bill's side. We hadn't seen each other in months, ever since that day I hollered that his mama won't shit. Tall and blonde and beautiful as ever, he turned to face me, his hair falling across his eyes as it had so many times on that futon: long humid nights, no AC but plenty of beer, a bucket of ice propped up in front of a box fan. Tangled in sheets, bending the frame. Goddamn. Some love doesn't end. Some love thrives forever in vaults we shove behind the shelves of our hearts, waiting only to be opened when alone, to come wild and alive again, knocking you down like the ocean.

But now, as we looked at one another, I saw that his eyes had changed. That gaze he'd gifted me on those long hot nights, open, warm, searching—

That gaze—was gone.

In its place, he looked—scared.

"Remember me?" I said, grinning, hoping to ignite some flame.

"Yes."

He shifted, looked nervously around the restaurant.

I opened my arms for a hug.

He backed away.

"Lindsay, it's great to see you, but—"

Suddenly, a blonde girl appeared at his side. A jealous brat, unattractive, unworthy. *Who is this bitch, and why is she wrapping her arms around him?* She smiled at me, mean as hell, trembling with hate.

"I just want to thank you for Bill," she spat.

He will never love you like he loves me. He will never again in his life love anyone like he loves me.

"You're welcome," I answered, pretending that I was not reeling, that I was not seeing spots—let me grab the counter lest I slide to the floor and arrive again at this man's feet—

I searched Bill's eyes, calling them to mine. Sending our stories through my gaze. If I let all my love for you spill from my eyes, you will remember, baby, that walk in the rain, the flowers you picked for me, the magic you made. There's something about falling in love in the rain, isn't it? I suppose we were always doing that: falling in love in the rain. Change a few letters, and the word 'kiss' turns to 'kill.' That's the backside of the coin, the side we choose to ignore while in each other's arms, forestalling our payment for all this joy. And now, the bill is presented. And now, I pay. Look into my eyes. Do you remember that you made love to me on the floor, smelling of oregano and a beat-up Pontiac, for the first six weeks of our mad passion? Look at me, my love, and see me. See me, and you cannot deny me—

He cast his eyes downward, then darted them for an instant to mine.

"Pizza's up!" shouted the guy behind the counter. The angry blonde snatched the box and pulled Bill out the door.

I never in my life saw him again.

"No man is going to want a stripper," Mama told me, when she discovered my dark truth on the back porch that summer.

"Pay attention in school," she warned me. "Look at me," she said, "beauty don't last."

I wrote my heart out that year. When I remember this time in my life, what I remember most is a spiral notebook, and a blue pen, and an ache in my shoulder from propping myself up on my bed to pen poetry, possessed. In the streets below my apartment, other students partied, as responsible students should. Like them, I stayed up all night. Unlike them, I remained locked into my solitude, spilling my broken heart, uncontrolled, compelled, driven. I didn't decide: *I will write.* The words took hold of me, instead. I couldn't resist, couldn't stop. The pen was my voice, the notebook my friend, an ear for the things no one wanted to hear. I'd cried to my roommate already—too much. She cleared out of the room when I shuffled in. My cousin Meredith must have had her fill, as well. She'd never tell me—she was far too kind—but I knew. Mama got sadder than I did at my problems; conversations with her only amplified the pain. That spiral notebook, that pen and that solitude, became my home.

When Spring registration rolled around, I selected creative writing courses.

"I'd pay to read this," he said, sliding my story across the table: a tale of two lesbian teenagers who murder an infant. Around us, the whole joint was populated with students like me. Aside from the occasional homeless person mumbling over a cup of coffee, Dr. Moore was the only grown-up around. He looked to be about twenty-odd years my senior. His hair was long and he had an earring in one ear. The lines on his face spoke experience I had yet to possess. I knew little about how to write; my taste was undeveloped, my skill unfinished. Yet I was filled with blood that spilled out in words, and I couldn't close the wound.

"Really?" I asked. "You think it's good?"

"Good? I think it's great. A lot of cleaning up to do. But great."

He leaned over the table, slid a cigarette from my pack with a smile.

"You don't mind?"

Dr. Moore had actual books published which one could find at Barnes and Noble. He might as well have been God himself.

"Take as many as you want."

It had been scary to ask him to meet with me this second time. I didn't feel it owed to me. I'd already had my fifteen-minute private conference in his office, the one included for all students. As I sat in his office that afternoon, I'd looked around, imagined a similar life for myself: books on the shelves, a manuscript in the typewriter. Outside his door, my classmates waited their turn. What must that be like, to have a series of people lined up to listen to you? To respect you? I'd worn a blazer to the bar that night to prove my seriousness, to justify my use of his time.

I was twenty-three. Would be twenty-four before I knew it. Already getting old. Beauty fading. I'd found a wrinkle across my forehead weeks prior. Mama was right. I needed to pay attention in school. And so, I'd mustered up my courage that day in his office. Leaned over his desk, shot him a smile. *Do you like corny jokes?*

"Do you think—we could meet again sometime?"

He grinned, kicked back.

"Sure," he said. "Thursday night?"

When I arrived at the bar, I found Dr. Moore in the back, two beers sitting on the table. "This round's on me," he said. I knew then that he would be receptive to my questions.

"Do you think I could become a professional writer?"

"You're talented," he said, "but the talent's raw. Untrained. Your use of adverbs, for example. The glut of information we don't need. Does anyone really care what color shirt your character is wearing? These are rookie mistakes. Writing is a craft, Lindsay. It's the *craft* you need to master."

"And then?"

And then—there's no telling what you could create. *Will* create."

"How do I do it? How do I learn the craft?"

"Well," he said, "you could go to grad school."

After I tried to end my life, I dedicated my heart to the Lord. I wasn't allowed visitors in the mental ward.

Nonetheless, one night, my sister-in-law found her way in.

She probably sweet-talked the nurses with that tiny voice of hers.

She had a soft spot for wounded birds, as she was one herself: she'd lost her brother to a tragic death at a young age; her mama's love was crazy and mean—there was a whole story to all of that. But you'd never hear it. This woman needed love, the wife of my eldest brother, but she was too innocent to recognize her own need. Instead, she saw only the needs of others.

They say hurt people hurt people.

But sometimes, hurt people heal people—

Or at least—they try.

And so, one night, disallowed, my sister-in-law found her way into the psychiatric ward, crawled right into bed with me, and saved my soul.

"Me and your brother sinned, too," she whispered, "before we said 'I do.'"

But there was hope, she explained. Jesus didn't get mad. Jesus understood. Jesus wept. Jesus forgave.

"Even though you feel like you're in big trouble, there is no trouble with God. You are forgiven the moment you are saved. But—Lindsay—*are* you saved?"

"I—I don't know."

"You can get saved right now."

She squeezed my hand.

A single tear sped down her cheek.

And that's how, in the dark of a hospital ward for the insane, I invited Jesus into my heart.

Someone had come to me in that black night. No anger. No punishment.

I thought that person was Jesus.

Now I realize—that person was actually my kind-hearted sister-in-law.

Nonetheless, she sold me on the Lord.

After I was released from the hospital, I promised myself that I'd stop having sex. The Bible was very clear about that rule. So I surrounded myself with the right people: a darling tender-hearted boy with the sleepy eyes and southern drawl of Elvis, a boy in the heat of puberty whose love for the Lord was rivaled only by our pulsating biology. His family, evangelical Christians, took me under their wing when other families shunned me: I was troubled, and thus *trouble*, but this clan was missionary to the core, swooping in on the vulnerable with kindness and indoctrination—good intentions, bad ideas. However, to a teenage pariah no longer invited to birthday parties, this sweet evangelical boy and his church became home. Together, twice weekly we attended services that operated in a warehouse where people wept and waved hands while a homespun Christian rock band played on stage. Sometimes, people hollered. Always, they cried. Each Sunday, sinners were invited to the stage to repent.

I was saved no less than seven times that year.

My evangelical Elvis and I considered purchasing purity rings, but our outside interests in the skateboarding set kept us from crossing that line into dangerously uncool. The cool kids smoked cigarettes behind Dumpsters on lunch break: we couldn't humiliate ourselves before them, these taste-makers of John M. Langston Junior High. My evangelical Elvis and I straddled worlds—attracted to the punk rock poetry of outsiders like me, yet enamored with the heavenly assurances of church folks like him.

Jesus would always love you. These dudes smoking cigarettes behind Dumpsters didn't promise you shit.

My evangelical Elvis and I straddled each other, too—my god, how could we resist, we were both young and ripe. After Sunday service, in his parent's basement, sweating through church clothes, we bathed one another in kisses we knew damn well we had no right to indulge. "Maybe you should wear longer skirts," he whispered, as he ran his hand up my thigh, pulling aside my underwear. He put the tips of his fingers in his mouth afterwards and sucked, savoring the taste of my body. Intensely erotic. I was drunk. I dug blindly into his dress khakis. He shuddered, moaned. Power. Afterwards, we prayed. And we promised: never again. We promised, purity rings—damn the popularity!

And then a new Pearl Jam album would come out, and the purity rings would take a back seat to JNCO jeans and chain wallets and the back of the Dumpster, cigarettes and angst and skateboard tricks that, sometimes, seemed more impressive than God.

I am one thing, and then I'm another, and I can't understand how these things can exist in tandem. I have understood one side of me to be light, good, the proper thing to do: collecting compliments from professors, collecting degrees, looking both ways before crossing the street. I have understood the other side of me to be dark, my wounds weaponized using forbidden tools: selling sex to gain my own esteem, begging men for approval as a pastime and a profession. To this day, I don't know where the truth about me lies. "I contain multitudes," I tell my husband when he points out the incongruities in my behavior. How can I strip on Sunday and teach at the university on Monday? I cite multitudes to comfort myself as much as convince him. It has been a long life of being horrified at who I am.

Now, when I look back at the events of my existence, the evidence on the table, it seems I am thoroughly everything, no neat categories within which I can place myself whole. A leg here, a heart there, stitched together in a tapestry mimicking wholeness, but in reality made of many parts, like those optical-illusion photographs that appear to be solid, complete, a single image—perhaps, a picture of a woman's face—but when you look closer, you realize: no, this is a mosaic of many portraits. Thousands of faces make up this larger one, yet only when up close can you see the disorder. Step back, and a single face emerges whole again. Could it be that the image is at once a single woman's face *and* a million others, as well? Could it be that they are both equally the truth?

I was feeling good for the first time in a long time when Sheena approached my stage. Thomas had relented his attention ever since the night of my successful evasion. I never knew why he stopped coming to the club; I chose not to ask. In his absence, I felt free, joyful. My white dress glowed in the blacklight as I spun on the stage. My wig swished across my back. Men gathered at my feet. I was plump and young—thought I was fat and old—yet those stage lights could convince even me of my worth. I lit up this room. Fuck everything I'd lost. I was good at losing. I saw in my reflection that woman on the pedestal, scrawled in Blue Cyan. This is who I have always been. This is who I will always be.

Into that woman on the stage, I buried my broken heart.

That star in the mirror engulfed my pain.

I could love her, and she loved me back.

I was in this state of rapture when Sheena approached me.

"I'm going out after work tonight," she said. "Wanna come?"

Yes, she had passed me on to a dangerous client. Yes, I felt betrayed, scared even, of who she might be beneath "Sheena." Sheena was, of course, not her real name. Her real name, I would never know.

And yet still I loved her. Lusted after her. Wanted her. Her, at her best. Her, at six foot two. Her, as power, as beauty, as everything they told us we could not be, transformed into one thousand dollars. I wanted to bask in her glory—and her glory alone, nothing less. The uglier side, I wished she'd keep hidden. I needed her shine to prove that I could shine too.

"I'd love to come," I answered.

By the time I reached the dressing room, Sheena was already gone.

But she'd left me a note.

Meet me at Europa.

Europa was a fashionable cocktail bar hidden underground, a dark space with leather couches and electronic music and wealthy twenty-somethings going about the important business of defining hipness.

However, as in the dressing room I pulled off my wig and changed into my street clothes, I realized in horror:

I have only sweat pants and a T-shirt to wear to this hipster bar.

I found the blazer I'd worn to meet Dr. Moore wadded in the back seat of my car. I pulled it on over the T-shirt, tucked the shirt into the sweatpants. Perhaps I could convince the bourgeoise that this was a new look? Yet as I walked through the hall of mirrors that marked the entryway to the club, in my reflection I saw only a ratty ponytail. A shapeless form. No long hair swinging. No white dress glowing. I would light up no rooms here.

I wanted to hide.

But it was too late.

"Lux," Sheena hollered, "join us!"

Curled up in a corner with some middle-aged dude wearing sunglasses, Sheena awaited.

As I approached, Sunglasses looked me up and down, taking in my unkempt appearance, and then shot a glance at Sheena. They burst into laughter.

"I didn't have anything else to wear."

"I can see that," she said.

Sheena patted the couch next to her and I sat down. She smiled big at me. Sheena didn't normally smile big. Sheena was hard underneath. But now, she seemed all goo under her skin. Ebbing. Bouncing. She couldn't sit still. Sheena rocked back and forth, working her jaw.

"I just—want to tell you—how much I love you," she said through gritted teeth. Taking my face into her hands, she touched the tip of her nose to mine. Sunglasses kicked back, grinning at the scene.

"I—love—you," she repeated.

She loved me? Was this real or a trick? I looked into her eyes, black with dilation. I wanted her to love me. I wanted to stand next to someone great. She'd taken me in since day one. Country like me. Hard like me. Hurt like me. Better than me. Advanced. *Sheena is our top earner!* I tilted my head, stupid, and pressed my mouth to hers. She sucked on my bottom lip for a moment before letting go.

"Hey," Sunglasses interrupted, placing a hand on my leg. "Want some Ecstasy?"

I looked to Sheena, licking her lips, rubbing her thighs, rocking. Her eyes fluttered backwards into her skull.

She didn't love me.

Sunglasses gave my leg a squeeze. "Sheena said you like to party?"

Every time I convinced myself that somebody loved me, I was wrong.

I wanted her to kiss me back and mean it. I wanted to feel big in her eyes, big by her side. I needed *that* Sheena. But this Sheena—blasted on E, giggling in some old dude's lap off-hours—this Sheena was not the one I wanted. This was not the Sheena that reflected the me I wanted to see. I needed her to be proud, strong, perfect. All light. No dark. I needed her to be what I needed her to be so that I could think myself okay, as I carved from another woman a pretty picture of myself.

I'm no better than Sunglasses. No better than any of these men.

I'm consuming her, too.

As I walked past the mirrors on my way to the door, I winced at my reflection. I always did have thin hair. Stupid outfit, a goddamned embarrassment. I turned my face away, couldn't look, didn't want a me that didn't shine, didn't want a me that wasn't *her*. The woman in Blue Cyan. The one on the pedestal. Another god of my making.

I'm consuming *her*, too.

Dr. Moore's words rang in my head.

"You're talented. There's no telling what you could create."

I fantasized a life that looked something like his:

A wood-paneled office at the university. Three framed degrees. A photo of a family, a stack of books, an award on the wall for Excellent Writing. Outside my door, young poets await. They love my novels. I'm an artist. Life has been hard. But with each blow, I have comforted myself with a promise: *at least this will make a good story.* Those stories, paid for dearly, now pay me back. I am not a fuck-up. Somebody wants me. Lots of people want me. I am respectable. Legitimate. A professor in a wood-paneled office.

I would spend the next three months writing personal statements and taking practice tests for the Graduate Records Exams. When I went into work, I avoided Sheena. She avoided me right back. Upon the chasm between us, we painted a benign veneer: she is with a customer and that's why she doesn't look at me; I am gluing my lashes and that's why I don't say hello. *I'm too busy, so sorry*, we tell the people we can no longer face, too afraid to say why, too proud to investigate the feelings behind our discomfort.

I couldn't forget the day we met. The straightness of her spine, the way the other girls deferred to her. *This is someone*, I'd thought, as she set up camp at the prime spot at the mirror. I couldn't forget her hands on my body, tying her thong into the most intimate parts of me. No man could ignore her on the floor. No woman could compete with her acumen. I couldn't forget who she had been to me. What she stood for. What her very existence had promised.

And yet, I also could not forget the working of the jaw. The love that wasn't real. The way she shrank when she removed her hair. Imperfections. Stains on the fantasy. If she was not the picture I'd painted, the illusion I'd created, what, then, was I?

Something had switched inside.

My mama calls it the Burton Coldness.

"Your daddy could turn off his heart just like pushing a button," she has often said.

Hearts must be turned off, doesn't she know? She does *not* know, and thus she has spent a life swimming in pain. If I had the Burton Coldness, Mama had the Shelton Despair. I'd rather turn to ice than a river of tears.

So I turned my heart off to Sheena. No longer did I see her power, her beauty, the length of her stride, the sparkle of her eye. Instead I thought ungenerous thoughts. *Where are your children? Are you so addicted to hoeing that you ruin everything else? Pathetic, to need the eyes of these men. Why do you ride home each night with a man who yells at you? Perhaps he yells at you because you do drugs with old dudes on your off-time.* These judgments against her: a protection for myself. As long as I could focus on her flaws, I could ignore my own. The things I hated in her—were those I feared in myself. By distancing myself from her—I distanced myself from me.

I started to pick myself apart in those stage mirrors. Nobody has hair this long, lashes this thick. No one has a smile this wide, a body this open, yesses forever on their lips. Fake. Unreal. Unclean.

Stupid, to have thought she loved me.

Stupid, to have thought I loved her.

I applied to graduate schools far away.

When we'd find a moment alone in the church closet, my Evangelical Elvis would pull me close and kiss me with the conviction he usually reserved for Jesus.

I'm sorry we did this again. Can we do this again?

"No one has ever done this to me," he whispered in the back of his parents' minivan, his hand on my breast, his fingers finding my nipple beneath my bralette.

"I'm sorry," I answered, pushing my body harder against his.

"We have to stop," he begged, as his mother piloted us through Danville to the tune of Joel Osteen, clueless.

"I'll walk you inside," he announced as we pulled up to my house.

We fled to my bedroom, feigning a lie about a forgotten piece of homework. As his mother waited in the driveway, as my parents waited downstairs, we made love feverishly in the space between the bed and wall before he pushed me off and came on my carpet. "Your body felt like a thousand lips," he said, spellbound and terrified, before he fled back to the minivan. The engagement took all of three minutes.

He called me that night to say we had taken it too far. And though I knew Jesus would agree, I couldn't stop smelling him on my body. I longed for the electricity in my spine to cease. I asked Jesus to erase the imprint of his hands on my hips. I prayed on my belly, rocking rhythmically against my fist even as I begged God to make it stop.

"A friend and I are…fornicating," I later confessed to my sister-in-law.

"Well, you know what you need to do."

"Stop?"

Consequences of fornication could include: teen pregnancy, maiming disease, righteous shame, another suicide attempt.

"How could you forget," she asked, "what got you into all this trouble in the first place?"

University of Louisiana said yes.

When the acceptance letter arrived, I wasted no time announcing my new station.

Even though it wasn't my shift, I drove straight to the Styxx and walked right onto the floor in my street clothes. I found Sheena instantly, cuddled with a customer; after all, I knew her hiding places. "Excuse us," I said to her customer, approaching their table. "Do you mind if I steal her for a minute?"

"What's up?" she asked as we walked away.

"I'm going to grad school. I'm leaving. It's over for me here."

"Congratulations," she told me, examining her fingernails.

"Thanks."

"You'll do great."

"Yeah."

"Better this way."

"Yeah."

Although I agreed with her well-wishes, nonetheless some part of my heart ached. Hush, ache, hush. You don't need her to beg you to stay. We are moving on to better things.

I pulled the acceptance letter out of my jacket pocket and placed it on the table between us.

She took it into her hands, read the words that meant my life here was ending.

"No good stripper ever says retire," she smiled, looking up from the letter.

"Maybe I'm not a good stripper."

"Don't be ridiculous," she said. "You are the best stripper the Lord ever made."

She reached across the table, grabbed my hand.

"Are you scared?" she asked.

Sheena's customer approached, wanting his turn. "Done yet?" he asked me, a fool. These men had no clue about us. No knowledge that behind the make-up, guts pumped. Tears did not glow in the blacklight. There were a lot of things these bastards would never see. Sure, I'm done, you fucking asshole. Done with this place. Done with everything and everyone in it. Done with Sheena. Done with Lux. Done with motherfuckers like you. I gave way to the customer, let him have my seat.

I can't be sure, because the room was dark, and my mind makes up stories, and a pretty woman hides her pain, but I think I saw Sheena mouth the words "I love you" as she watched me walk away.

As I strode the club floor for the final time, I reminded myself to take it all in, imprint this place in my memory. Around me, a sea of dancers swirled, a current of rhinestones and starshine running through the deepest, darkest ditch downtown. In the middle of this bedlam I stood, sporting a spiked dog collar and leather jacket, a kid in a suit of armor holding in her hands the herald of her redemption. School would cure me. School would save me. *Don't you remember what got you into all this trouble in the first place?*

The manager appeared by my side, plucked at my leather jacket.

"You got no business on the floor wearing some shit like this."

"It's not my shift."

"Well, do you want it to be? We're short on girls."

I looked around the room. Women rising from chairs. Men following them like dogs. The lap dance room was hopping.

"There's good money to be made here tonight," he said.

And wasn't good money always the best excuse?

Maybe I wasn't ready for goodbye.

Maybe—I never would be.

"I'll stay," I said. "One last time."

As I applied make-up at the dressing room counter, I admired my beauty. Fresh and young, as if nothing had ever happened to me. Eyes still sparkling, no dark circles yet. My life would only start to tell on me in my thirties. For now, I was safe. Sweet. Untouched. Indeed, even beneath the foundation and the eyeshadow, the youth and beauty held; skin scrubbed, I was still a sunrise on the mountain. Yet the innocence—was an illusion. Beneath the skin churned hideousness unseen: a worn woman, beaten and alone and grasping. Maybe not a woman. Maybe, still a kid. This life—this club—these men—this make-up: everything I'd been warned against becoming. *Becoming*, as if I'd ever been anything other than exactly this.

"Are you scared?" Sheena had asked me, and I never got the

chance to answer. I wasn't scared of going to grad school, I'd like to tell her. I was scared of staying here. Scared of myself.

"You're not wearing that on your last shift," Sheena said, as she entered the dressing room to find me stepping into an old teddy. "You done rubbed all the polka-dots off."

She was right. Innumerable hours sliding my body against customers had worn patches in the high traffic areas. My breasts, my belly, my ass: all bald.

"You ought to care how you look on your last night," she said.

She pulled her trunk from beneath the counter, the words "Sheena DO NOT TOUCH" spray painted across the front. Diving elbow-deep into a mass of garters and thongs, she reemerged with a sequined two piece.

"Remember this?"

I stared at the outfit. Of course I remembered it, the first act of love she'd ever shown me, this bikini she had tied onto my body before I'd ever once walked the floor. I didn't know what she meant by this kindness now, didn't know where we stood, what we felt. *Sheena, do not touch.* I was afraid to attribute real feelings to us. Our relationship was born in a house of smoke and mirrors. I didn't even know her real name. Never would.

There was a whole big world I'd never known, right here in this woman.

Nudity simulates intimacy. I'd seen all of Sheena, watched her shave her ass crack, watched her insert a tampon. Yet when it came to our names, our histories, where we went when the lights came on—over these matters of the heart we stretched a silence still and calm as the skin of a lake, hiding a fathom of unspeakable creatures within—afraid of ourselves, afraid of each other.

"Go ahead," Sheena urged. "Put it on."

As she fastened her top around my ribcage, she nodded toward the mirror.

"Tell me," she asked, "what do you see?"

Flesh, supple and full. A collection of guts, housed in a candy-coated shell. Imperfect parts positioned in strategic pose to approximate perfection. An illusion and a feast. In my leather jacket piled upon the floor below: a letter of acceptance, a new life, the direction I was supposed to go.

I would forget about that tonight.

Tonight, I would believe the magic. I would swoon over my reflection, a goddess on a pedestal, a woman I had conjured into being. I would say yes to her, one last time. I spun in the mirror and smiled. I think I'll miss her, that woman on the pedestal. She had taken my pain and smiled back. She had swallowed. She had survived.

Sheena stepped back, looked me over. In her eyes I saw a sadness pass. But as quickly as that sadness came, it disappeared.

"Did you ever wonder what happened with Thomas," she asked; "did you ever wonder why he never came back?"

I remembered the night in Europa. The customer she'd inexplicably joined on her off-time. What does it take to get a regular, I'd asked her, a lifetime ago, before things got so complicated. She wouldn't answer me then. Sheena undertook labor I'd never see; Sheena did things she'd rather not tell me about. I'd thought she was protecting herself, her own image. Could it be that she had been protecting me? Could it be that Sunglasses wasn't the only customer Sheena entertained on her off-time? I struggled to answer her question, to say the right thing, to dare speak what I was thinking: she had taken Thomas back so I wouldn't have to. She had loved me, after all. She had taken the fall. But for all my good intentions, I could not get the truth out of my mouth.

"Good luck, Lux," she smiled as she walked away.

"Wait."

She stopped in the doorway, an inch away from disappearing from my life forever.

"My name is Lindsay. I always wanted you to know that."

"You told me your name the day we met," she said. "I haven't forgotten. Have you?"

Fred lasted two weeks in the cage.

I wanted him to be content, but he wasn't.

At first, he was restless. A taste of the outdoors had clued him into the possibilities embedded in his DNA. The cage was too small for a creature with wild ambitions. Untold generations of feral animals poured through his veins, commanding him to leap, to scale, to tear through our home as if it were a forest. Yet we had disabled him with our human hands. The comforts of our home—a warm place to sleep, kibble on demand, heights no greater than the china cabinet on the best of days—had stolen from him the skills and courage to face the forest that called to him.

We are looking for a situation that fits us, a place in the world, a way of being that feels like home, but some of us will never find it. Our blood screams, *run*. Yet our mind whispers, *stay*. In our veins tear the lawless desires of the beasts, of nature, of God. Nonetheless we return to the locked door, the four walls, for they are all we have ever known. How could we understand that instinct would carry us through, if only we'd trust it? How could Fred know that he could leap from tree to tree? What if he'd never felt the warmth of a human's palm? What if he'd never tasted the nectar of the baby bottle? Could he forget the soothing sound of Chopin? Could he trust the blood in his veins?

He could not.

And so, he threw himself at our door, and back into a cage.

At first, he was restless.

Then, he became silent.

He seemed to understand the smallness of his surroundings, and ceased to pretend otherwise.

He laid down and stayed that way.

Placid, like a house cat.

I was pleased with his calm demeanor.

Until two weeks later, I awoke to find him stiff on his back.

Stretched out the length of the cage, eyes wide and tongue thrust from his mouth, Fred laid frozen in the grotesque pose of death. When I revealed the horrible scene to Daddy, he didn't poke Fred with a single finger, as I had. He didn't recoil, or scream, as I had.

Instead, he took Fred into his hands.

This dead squirrel—no longer pliable, no longer purring—had morphed into a corpse, a thing loathsome by most accounts. Nonetheless, Daddy held Fred under his chin, as tender as if he were still a blind baby in need of saving.

"I knew better than to cage him," Daddy said, "and I goddamn did it anyway."

PART TWO

CHAPTER EIGHT
After the Party is Over

In the morning, after the party was over, I surveyed the wreckage outside my home. Tangled streamers littered the parking lot; a label from a Miller Lite tumbled across the asphalt. In the apartment above: my husband, our son, a few small rooms containing exactly what I'd wanted. I knew I shouldn't feel sad. I knew this should be enough. Yet as my dogs sniffed at the remnants of my thirtieth birthday party, around me hung a fog.

Desire. Regret.

Everything I could no longer have.

When I went back to stripping, I was thirty years old, had a husband and a baby, and was knee-deep into a PhD. My husband worked long hours teaching high school English, spending his days on campus and his nights bent over the kitchen table planning classes. My baby became my best friend. His chubby fingers played in my hair as he fed from my breast, gazing up at me with my daddy's blue eyes—eyes I thought I'd never see again, after all these years, reborn, brand-new.

Or were those my husband's eyes?

My ass ached from sitting all day.

My nipples grew sore, and then numb.

I'd begged the universe for this family. This baby.

Drawn pictures of what I wanted in my diary.

First, of brides.

Then, pregnant women.

Using pills and prayers, I'd conjured into my barren womb the single pregnancy of my entire promiscuous life.

It took me three days of feral agony to give birth.

"No drugs," I'd instructed the doctors; "I trust my body."

On day two of labor, the midwife shoved her arm into my vagina, ripped open my cervix with a gush a blood, and told me to go walk around the Wal-Mart. I refused a C-section, resolved to push this child into the world as God intended. Indeed, I accomplished just that: seventy-two hours into labor and just three hours before my twenty-ninth birthday, on a Friday the thirteenth—an evil day by most accounts—I delivered my son into the hands of his father.

My father delivered me, too. However, unlike my husband, there were no doctors by his side. Mama told the obstetrician that the baby was on the way, but he didn't believe her. "You've got hours to go," the doctor said as he left the room.

"The baby's coming *now*," Mama growled at Daddy.

"Now, Linda, you know that can't be true," he replied.

Mama raised her legs.

"Well, the fuckin' head's out," she said.

And thus, in a hospital full of people that didn't believe my mama, my daddy's unpracticed hands brought me earthside.

By the time the nurses made it into the room, I was already in his arms.

And that's how, a lifetime ago, a blue-eyed man named David delivered me into this world—and then, twenty-nine years later, a blue-eyed man named David delivered my own child, as well. As the years have passed since our son's birth, I have hung on to this poetic parallel.

Growing up, my brothers were the stars. My eldest brother Michael, Daddy's son from his first marriage, kept everyone busy with his rampant hooliganism. When Michael wasn't in trouble with some girl, he was riding his bike off the roof. *Is that your brother,* the neighbor kids would ask, awed, as Mike struggled that bike out the second story window and sailed it across the sky.

My other brother, Jason, Mama's son from her first marriage, was a star, too. Dashingly handsome, the girls of Danville flocked to his baseball games. "Are you Jason Talbott's little sister?" they would ask me, twirling pigtails and popping gum, confused that we didn't share the same last name, confused that I wasn't stunning like him.

Where I come from, women occupy bleachers.

But my father—he saw me.

Daddy knew I didn't want to sit and clap. He knew I wanted my name on people's lips. The bleachers were no place for a person like me.

"You don't care about baseball," Daddy told me later, when I expressed my desire to play Little League. He was correct, yet tears sprung to my eyes. "You're an artist," he said, as he airbrushed my name across a shirt. "Artists are supposed to hurt."

I would become expert at this assignment.

Daddy brought me wild animals, creatures I could never keep. Before there was Fred, there were turtles, little stragglers he'd find crossing the road on his way to work. I'd awake in the morning to find a red-eared slider munching on a piece of lettuce in a shoe box filled with dirt. "Think he might need a friend," Daddy would tell me. For days, weeks even, I'd shower them with love, pour into these hard-shelled animals all the sweetness I had no other direction in which to give. But inevitably, the time would come for goodbye.

"You gotta set him free," Daddy would say.

"But I love him."

"Don't matter if you love him. Them woods are what he needs."

"You have this need to be…*seen*," my husband has remarked, from time to time. He says it like it's the strangest desire in the world: *to be seen.*

He isn't wrong about me. I'm addicted to being seen.

On stage, a woman all curves and mystery, her value evident by the money at her feet. Seen, a thirteen-year-old girl on her back in the woods. Seen, a teenage target for a man's fists. I've always felt shame around that desire. Who was I to be seen?

"You have this need to be seen," my husband told me, like it was the basest shit ever, and I can't help but judge in unison: yes, there is something wrong with me, something wrong with my desires.

I feed them anyway.

And that is why, facing the wall of my cubicle in between classes, pumping a breast with one hand and surfing the internet with the other, I planned my own thirtieth birthday party.

A party bus. A theme: Class to Trash. We would start the evening at the swankiest cocktail bar in the city and move down from there, ending finally at The Clermont Lounge, Atlanta's oldest strip club, the home of Atlanta's oldest strippers.

When my husband returned from work and relieved me of the baby, I would steal away into the bathroom for a hot shower, my sole luxury. Solitude. Sovereignty. Nobody needing me. Wiping the steam from the mirror, milk streaming down my belly, I searched for my face in the unfamiliar mask that greeted me in the mirror. Dark circles. Lines. Turning away from my reflection, I remembered: I had once been beautiful.

For a full nine months before baby came, no man would look at me, invisible, a taken vessel.

For a full year after baby came, my body, accustomed already to serving, now learned to serve in a new way. I'd quiet my baby with my breast and stare black-eyed into the night, my husband snoring peacefully by my side, everyone in the home asleep but me.

Once, there had been things I wanted. And I knew that all of this—this man by my side, this baby at my breast—were included in that list. However, I couldn't remember what else there'd been. Other desires? Surely there'd been other things?

"I am the sleep martyr," I told my husband when he got up the next morning.

"Well," he said, "I do have to be up early for work."

When our baby turned six months old, I stuffed myself back into a blazer, lined my bra with cotton, and returned to teaching Freshman Composition for peanuts, my position as graduate teaching assistant humble yet nonetheless hard-won. In a chaotic life, school had become a constant. The more degrees I obtained, the closer I got to a real life, some respectable existence I imagined for myself.

I spent my whole life trying to be someone who wouldn't get left.

It started with the animals. The turtles, the squirrel. Each of these beloveds, a wild creature that could be held only temporarily: nothing sturdy, a goodbye written on the other side of hello. But then, one day, Daddy brought home a dog. I was perhaps ten years old.

A storm raged outside when Daddy entered our home soaking wet. Branches from a dogwood slapped the window. A little black and brown puppy shivered in Daddy's coarse hands. It was dark outside, late. Daddy was heading out for work when he heard whimpering.

"Found him hiding under the car," Daddy said. "Someone must've dumped him."

Outside, thunder crashed.

"Well, bring him on in," Mama conceded. I leapt into the air, delighted. A puppy! An angel to call my own!

"We'll name him Raphael," I decreed.

"That ain't no name for a dog," Daddy said. "His name is Buster."

I resolved to make this dog mine.

"Feel the knot on his head?" Daddy asked, as the dog stretched up for Daddy's attention. "That's a smart knot. That's how you know a dog is intelligent."

I would prove just how clever he could be.

Each day, I would take Buster into the back yard, a glossy slice of American cheese in my hand. Within weeks, I had him sitting on command, awaiting a taste. Soon, I had him shaking my hand, his brown eyes alight as I fed him Kraft singles. Once, during our training period, the dog and I became locked outside. I rang the doorbell, and Mama let us in. After that, Buster learned to ring the doorbell himself. From then on, he could be let outside to do his business, no supervision necessary, and he would return promptly each time, ringing that bell with his great paw for entry.

Daddy was right—this dog was special.

On his front foot I found a sixth toe.

"Another sign of intelligence," Daddy advised, when I pointed out this anomaly.

As long as I could domesticate this puppy, I surmised, teach him to behave—I would never lose him.

Dave was from Milwaukee; I was from Danville; we met in Lafayette, Louisiana, two strangers in a strange land, where storefronts advertised live worms for sale, the bayou had been paved into a parking lot, and an alligator might just end up in your backyard. No ornate iron trellises awaited us, no swinging swamp juke-joints; instead, Spanish moss draped over a strip mall where live oaks used to grow. Lafayette—was not what either of us had expected from Louisiana. We bonded on that point first.

In most ways, Dave and I were opposites: piercings in my face and tattoos on my arms, I entered that English department a rebel with a cause. He showed up a corn-fed Midwesterner who'd never broken a rule. He said he wanted something different when he moved to the bayou. On that wish, I delivered.

Dave was my officemate, and he drove me nuts. While I focused on my work, head down and scribbling, he interrupted my writing by singing show tunes. He'd pop up beside my desk, chin in one hand, drumming his fingers on the tabletop with the other, and ask,

"Hey Burton, don't you want a smoke?"

Dave had never smoked a cigarette in his life, but he loved any excuse to kick off work with me.

He was wholesome. The epitome of untroubled. He had only been with one woman in his life—his current girlfriend. High school sweethearts standing the test of time, he kept a photo of them on vacation in London on his bookshelf. I judged her plain, unexciting—all round, no edges. She was born rich; her parents invested in her heavily; she had turned out brilliant and well-behaved. I was jealous of those opportunities. As Dave and

I worked on our Master's degrees, she began a career with the CIA. The two of them decided: Dave would live in Louisiana for these two years while she built a career in Washington, D.C.; he would move in with her when the degree was done.

I had my own boyfriend, a casual place holder who was not technically as impressive as Dave's girlfriend but who had liked me enough to move with me from Richmond to Louisiana. He wore blue-collar as a style, sporting homemade tattoos inked by a nodding-out junkie at a kitchen table in a trailer. He romanticized redneckism and therefore was perfectly happy for me to act as whorish as I wanted. This was a man who'd been raised nice in the suburbs, and consequently loved hardcore music and scars. Perhaps in me he saw darkness and danger and decided he wanted a taste. Yet as my life wheeled from stripper to scholar, I wanted more than ever to cut ties with the old. This alienation was not lost on him.

As I headed to class, he asked what my examination of literature added to society. "I make things," he said, a metalworker by trade. "What do you make?"

For the first time in my life, I occupied a community centered on high-in-the-head thoughts and grand ambitions. No one smoked crack at social gatherings. Instead, they discussed Foucault. My work environment no longer consisted of broken mirrors and bare women. In their place I found nerds in tweed. I didn't want to be the woman I had been. She frightened me. There were certain paths for personal ascension and one must eventually choose one. I had chosen, and now I wanted to play the part.

Dave's fondness for me further encouraged my desire for upward assimilation. If this patently-good man enjoyed my company, called me funny, read my poetry—what did that say about me? Dave had no concern for being cool, had even less interest in darkness. He wore Eddie Bauer shoes and sported the same haircut he'd had since he was five. He still wears that haircut, by the way. He contorted himself to fit no one's mold. He sought to impress no one.

That impressed me.

Each Thursday, the English department hosted literary readings to showcase grad student writers. When it was my turn to share my work, Dave sat up front. As I read my piece, a bitter tome about being unloved, he kept his eyes on me. Years later, well into our marriage, he would still remember some of my best lines. He was interested in me. Not just my body. Not just something to consume. As I read, and he listened, I felt as if I was pouring my heart into him. When he complimented my work afterwards, he poured my heart back into me.

I never expected a man to listen. We women hold stories unspeakable and unsexy. The threads of our life we unspin delicately, tentatively, and rarely, because no one likes a talkative woman; we've seen him fumbling with the salt shaker and looking at the door. He'll listen long enough to fuck you, but he's suffering through every minute. We get so used to being bodies. Bodies to adorn, manipulate, punish into attractiveness, earn the honor of ornamenting a man, an accessory to his greatness. I never learned to hook a man with a thorough display of myself. Never once believed the stuff of my heart deserved an audience, much less affection. Instead I twisted my body into an expression of availability. Mouth open. Legs spread. Short skirts. Is there any other way to earn his eyes, his esteem?

Yet Dave's unpretentiousness—as well as the necessary brevity of our friendship, limited by a two-year Master's program—altered my usual protocol of engagement. I didn't feel compelled to perform sex clown for him. Such a display felt unnecessary, and not the target of his interest in me, anyway. Not to mention, he had a girlfriend. I had a boyfriend. Nevermind that my boyfriend couldn't possibly be more turned off by my changing tastes.

I ached to be seen from the inside out.

I churned with life that spit out of my mouth in poems.

Dave sat in the front row and listened as I excavated my psychic tombs.

He loved the roiling depths of my wild heart before he ever touched my body.

"We are the best two," he told me one night, as a gang of us grad students ambled through downtown Lafayette. "You and me."

Later on, in a hallway of a bar, we found ourselves alone. He was heading home; could he hug me goodbye? Loose with whiskey, friendly with wine, we both held on longer than was proper. After all, my boyfriend sat only one room over, nursing a Pabst while he suffered through the egghead ramblings of my fellow scholars. A thousand miles away, Dave's girlfriend awaited his nightly phone call. In that moment, we cared about neither of them. Maybe it was the way the room stood still in his arms. Maybe the way he looked at me, so sweet. Those blue eyes. That gentle smile. This man who listens. This man who thinks I'm great. He's never seen me naked. I've given him nothing. And yet he wraps his arms around me tighter. He's got everything to lose. A whole big life out there. A woman he has loved since he was a boy. "I can't get enough of you," he whispered into my neck, and then pressed his mouth against mine.

"We kissed last night," he reminded me, first thing the next morning, his phone call rising me from bed.

"We don't have to make anything of it," I replied.

Our friendship would continue in this congenial manner until six weeks before we moved away from Louisiana and each other, when it erupted into an illicit affair.

"I might not get accepted at any of these programs," I told Dave, as outside our office I smoked cigarettes and worried over my scholastic fate. At that time, he and I were both making six hundred dollars a month as graduate assistants. The need to Do Something With My Life pressed upon me, and like many of my peers, I had begun the grueling process of doctoral program application.

"Come on, Burton! Where's the bravado?"

"I've got to get in somewhere, or I don't know who I am anymore."

"Don't worry," he smiled. "You'll remember pretty quickly."

The whole office was panicked. What does one do with a Master's degree in English except get more degrees? "Have you heard anything," I'd ask my colleagues each morning, examining their faces for clues.

Again and again, they came: the rejection letters. Hauling ass across my apartment complex to the mailbox, hand trembling as I turned the key to discover another thin envelope, terror for my future choked my throat, causing me rush to the bathroom and anxiety-puke until exhaustion calmed my heartbeat.

Until one day, huffing and puffing, I discovered a thick envelope.

Six rejection letters in one week, and one acceptance letter today.

Georgia State.

I am moving to Atlanta.

I rushed into my apartment to share the good news.

"I did it!" I told my boyfriend. "I'm going to be a doctor!"

He raised his hands and clapped slow, his eyes empty, an extreme display of apathy. Without a word, he left for work.

I called Dave.

"I got into a PhD program," I sobbed. "Georgia State. I'm moving to Atlanta."

"Congratulations," he said. "But why are you crying?"

"Because my boyfriend hates me."

"Come over," he replied.

An hour later I knocked on his door, face smeared with mascara, clothed in the house rags of the depressed. "The future Dr. Burton," he announced, pulling from behind his back a bottle of champagne. He popped the cork, bottle spraying. I squealed, laughed, my shirt wet.

I never liked champagne, but I drank deeply of this gift.

The nagging panic was over. The uncertainty. A change was coming.

That was the day I fell in love with my husband.

I spent the night at his apartment and didn't leave for a week.

Falling in love with Dave was sweet and forbidden. I was everything he shouldn't do, ripped jeans and tattoos. He was everything I hadn't wanted—straight-laced and stable, a square with a future. We held hands under tables. We kissed at bars when no one else was looking. We were lonely and scared and starving for a friend. In a mere month and a half, we would both move. I would move to Atlanta; he would move in with his real girlfriend in DC. My heart curdled with jealousy against her. I dressed up that jealousy as superiority. Unlike her, I was exciting, interesting! Unlike her, I'd had nothing handed to me!

Including this man.

Whom I would make mine.

During the week I spent at Dave's apartment, I barely changed out of my depression jammies. My shirt was worn, threadbare, covered in tiny holes. Through one of these holes, a nipple poked out. This was not lost on me.

Nor him.

By midweek, I had him locked between my thighs.

I never thought I would love like this again. Such doomed delicious passion, one can only expect once in a lifetime. Yet here, in Dave's apartment, again I found fury, tenderness, interludes on the floor. Kisses so crazed they bruised my lips. You must leave soon. Kiss me harder. I love the goodbye as much as the hello. Agony carries its own pleasure, a promise in the pain: this must be love, this must be beauty, because it hurts so bad to lose.

He didn't want to betray his girlfriend. Anxiety surged through him at the slightest rule breached. His guilt plagued him, but stronger than his regret was my erotic power. I had cast the spell. He was done for.

He and I often joked that I was poisonous.

He once lost feeling in his finger for days. Another time, he pulled a muscle in his tongue. Back then it was fun to tell him, *I'm poisonous*. It was—good God we're so hot for each other that we're hurting each other. One of my favorite memories is when he shoved his heavy coffee table out of our way as we slid from the futon to the floor, his mouth on my throat. Hunger. He's the only man who's ever bruised my lips.

He resisted intercourse, although each night at his apartment grew increasingly feverish. He felt that boundary to be the unbreachable betrayal he would not commit. I begged in ways irresistible. How anyone could say no was beyond me, yet for three nights in a row, he did. But on the fourth night, he folded.

Afterwards, he escaped to his bedroom, where he spent the night alone, leaving me on his futon. I was illicit, not allowed. He was appalled at himself for cheating. Horrified. The man loves rules. His heart pounds when he breaks them.

The next day, he asked if my feelings were hurt, and I choked out a yes. I was embarrassed. Ashamed.

We would both leave soon. There was no point in starting up some dumb doomed love. On that point, we agreed. But by the end of the conversation about how we needed to stop this train, my throat was covered in hickeys, my lips purple from kisses. Ravaged. Furious.

I stayed at his apartment as days turned into a week. He made me dinner, white chicken chili, the first of thousands of meals he would cook for me in this life. We watched every episode of *The Office*. I washed his dishes, even though I don't do dishes. I only returned to my empty apartment occasionally, to walk the dogs. Neglected animals, locked in crates. Neglected bills. Neglected preparations for my move. I was in love and obsessed.

During the six weeks that spanned our affair, I wrote like a madman, compelled, my art my only comfort. Alone in my apartment, falling wildly in love with Dave just in time to lose him forever, horror plucked my eyes open at three in the morning and set me before a glowing screen. Wine-drunk in the middle of the night, my fingers hammered out my cursed heart, the tale of our love accompanied by the sound of a ticking clock. The end was set when this began. Yet he couldn't get enough of me. He called each morning when he woke up, and he called each night before he went to bed. He kissed me so sweetly in that hallway. He showed up at my place with a milkshake on a Tuesday. He's the only man who's ever bruised my lips.

Many years later, now his wife, I searched through the works I'd written during our wild love. As I scanned the pages, I discovered the words "don't go" repeated throughout, an unconscious chant, the refrain of my pleas.

An affair means passion. Sex. Interstate hotel rooms. No yawning in front of a television. A movie blaring in the background, and you don't see a thing, don't hear a line. Underwear slung across the back of a couch. The inevitable goodbye.

Love feels like nothing without the inevitable goodbye.

Graduation loomed ever closer. Our time together ran ever shorter.

And yet—I sought him out.

Once, in my parking lot, after an hour of making out in his car, I blurted out "I feel like I love you," a half-assed confession blurred within tears, too afraid to just outright say it, defenseless in the dark.

"There is no future in this," he replied.

Dave was good. Righteous. Correct.

I, on the other hand, was raised under the notion that an affair meant true love.

My parents' marriage began illicitly, of course.

Legendary scenes of their early romance include: Daddy battling Steve in the parking lot outside the movie theater; Daddy slinging a tire iron against Steve's head; a hospital stay for Steve, maybe jail for Daddy—and then me, on the way. My conception: the fruit of violence and broken rules.

An affair means losing your mind. It feels good. You can just—let loose a little.

Like most affairs, my parents' was luxury in the midst of deprivation. Steve treated Mama bad: slept around, slung her around. Daddy was fancy with turquoise jewelry. My mama likes nice things and entirely believes she deserves them. My daddy couldn't pass a mirror without looking twice.

Daddy was Steve's friend and employee at the Gypsum factory. In sympathy for Daddy's recent divorce, Steve told Mama, well, we ought to invite David over for dinner.

"That's the last time I ever invite a man over for meatballs," Steve would later vow.

When Mama met Daddy, he was a charismatic alcoholic clad in a be-bop hat and long necklaces. He was a decade older than Mama in years that suggested eternal loyalty. A man like him doesn't leave a woman like her. And a woman like her doesn't leave a man like him.

Mama had just watched *A Star is Born*, and as across the dinner table she listened to Daddy talk, she imagined his gravelly voice as that of Kris Kristofferson, and she dreamed herself Barbara Streisand, just inches away from fame and tragedy. My mother imagines life more worthwhile if a dark sad danger looms just around the corner from joy.

But she didn't like Daddy at first because she considered him a bad influence on her first husband, who sometimes stayed out until the next morning, or even for days, and didn't bother to call.

Initially, she only kissed Daddy to teach Steve a lesson.

After the meatball dinner, the legend goes, Daddy started making excuses to visit. One day he showed up because he'd forgotten his sunglasses. He knew Steve would be at work at that time. Mama knew what that meant. She allowed him to kiss her, in her mind the mantra, *I will only do this once.*

I forgive him, but not me.
I forgive me. But not him.
I resolved to forget us. But I can't.

If I could stop writing about him, I would.

Five days left. So much to pack. Phone calls to make. We leave on the same day. Drive in the same direction. But I'll stop. And he'll drive on.

Five days left, and I want to be with him all the time. I must find a way to hate him. Perhaps first, I'll cook him dinner.

The night we leave Louisiana, I will drive to Danville, seek refuge at Mama's house. It will be my first night of truly being without a man—something I've put off. Sure, I've been living by myself, but there's always been him to kiss. Occasional orgasms. Phone calls—lots of them. I stayed at his apartment for a week and I haven't been the same ever since. I got a new boyfriend. My new boyfriend just didn't get a new girlfriend.

Without some form of intoxication, I will never be able to sleep that night. I will beg Mama for benzos and compensate with my tastefully framed Master's degree. Yet still I must rise the next day, and mornings are the worst. I wake panicked, daily. I can talk myself out of the foolishness after I have smoked some weed and talked to Meredith. But the first thing I think upon waking these days is Oh Shit.

I rationalize our situation in various forms. For instance: he got cold feet and he wanted to have a bad girl experience—a wild oats scenario. Or, he hasn't seen his girlfriend in a long time; my boyfriend broke up with me; I was available, and he was itchy, and we filled some space for each other—mainly situational. Another option is, I am so entrancing that he couldn't resist falling in love with me, and his feelings for me will haunt him for years, if not totally change his life.

I like that last one.

Mama tells me there's no good in looking back. No point. I resolve to stop rationalizing. I will not call him once I move. How can I speak to him knowing that he's just slept with another girl?

I don't care that it's his girlfriend. If I'm going to have a man, I want to goddamn have him. Once we move, I resolve, I will not call him.

I got a cell phone today, and later, after he was briefly at my apartment, I noticed that he had entered himself into my contact list. He senses my resolve. For a moment, his is the only name in my phone. Immediately I start adding people. He calls and interrupts me; he says he should've stayed over longer.

He doesn't want to leave without saying goodbye. He tells me he'll call me every day. But I've faced it: our relationship is over in five days. He wants to wean off of me. He still wants me in his life. But this—this now—this hot, silly, sad doomed relationship— this is me in his life. I cannot go back to the Lindsay who flirted but didn't kiss, who laughed and expected nothing. We have kissed. I don't expect nothing. I'm getting nothing. I can't forgive that. I have to move on somehow.

He caught me when I was vulnerable. He bought me champagne when I got into a PhD program. He allowed me to fall in love with him, yet he steeled himself against me. So what that he warned me? I knew he was unavailable. And yet he continued to cultivate within me a love for him. He consistently left me one inch from satisfied, and sometimes I think he enjoyed that. Now he's leaving me to pretend like this never happened.

I knew he had a girlfriend. I knew he was moving in with her. The time limit was set before this began. And yet—I sought him out. I kept my pussy shaved. I always tried to look pretty if he was going to be around. I wrote love letters stained with tears for a man who had long armored himself with frank assertions of his lack of future expectations.

We couldn't resist. We were best friends. He made me laugh. He liked my accent. He listened to my poetry. I put his name under my pen. My wildness read as adventure, a dazzling cave to explore.

We lived together for one week. One night, long ago, a month and a half and a chasm away, we kissed drunk at a bar. When he pulled away, I held my eyes closed to hold the moment still. Sometimes, I still keep them closed after he kisses me. It's been so long since I've felt good. And it's just like I predicted—we will continue this doomed relationship until he walks out of my door. We will kiss goodbye. We will kiss until it is irrevocably goodbye.

Don't go.

Don't go.

Don't go.

Five days later, Dave packed up everything he owned, stacked his life in a compact car, tossed in the Dumpster what wouldn't fit—what didn't make the cut. The next morning, he would drive across the country to his real life and his real girlfriend. "Don't bother saying goodbye to me," I'd warned him.

He was mine for six weeks, and then he wasn't.

But before he left town, he showed up at my door.

"I had to see you once more."

How could he leave me? How could he move in with her after what had happened? How could he forget this love? Wasn't he, too, cursed by this love? *Time*, he told me, *time*—time will make it better. But what did he know about being left? What did he know about that kind of time?

Daddy died, and I learned not to trust. Don't get comfortable. Be afraid. Men disappear. Next, I yoked myself to a madman who nonetheless intoxicated me. I begged him for his love even while he pummeled me with his fists. After that, I found joy at last in Bill, yet I was so stained by pain that I poisoned our love, and he left too. *Time*, Dave told me, *time will make this better*, but what did he know about being left? What did he know about that kind of time?

As before me he wept through a goodbye, I tried to conjure anger against him. I had prepared to enact a cold dismissal should he arrive at my door. *Fine*, I would tell him; *leave*. Leave me and go to her. This has been goodbye from the moment it was hello. I could've killed somebody with my rage, then. I had done everything in my power to steal him. Performed my ultimate sexual tricks when allowed the opportunity. Once, I even washed his dishes. I shaved my legs for the most mundane of events. None of this had worked to secure his love. Instead he would drive one thousand miles to move in with another woman, a rich girl guaranteed to put him to sleep. I had no compunction about undermining her. I knew she loved him.

But I loved him too.

And I had one tool left in my belt.

As in each other's arms we said our final goodbye, I put it out there. Gave him the option I had been too proud to ever speak.

"If you change your mind, you can come to me."

A light leapt into his eyes.

"Plans mean nothing," I continued. "Anything can happen. It already has."

And then, I placed into his hand all of the things I'd written through the midnight fevers of the last six weeks. He took the folder and looked at me with the saddest farewell. He smiled, but his eyes held pools they could not contain. And then I watched, palm to the window, as he drove into the night and out of my life. He would tell me, later, he added an earring to that folder, a souvenir of mine he'd saved from our week together—only throwing it away when he got a few miles from his new home, when such pieces of me became too dangerous to contain.

I smoked cigarettes on Mama's back porch for three days as I waited to deny his call, hoping the phone would ring so I could refuse to pick it up. I yearned for him—yearned even to deny him. To reject him. To let the call go unanswered. To leave him, as he had left me. Yet, three days later, when he did call, I could not resist. He said, *help me,* and I said, *how?* He said, *meet me,* and I said, *where?* Then I curled my hair, bought some beer, and drove through the night to an interstate hotel room on the outskirts of Richmond, the incidental halfway point between Danville and DC. During the day, we walked through Carytown, fingers interlaced, sharing an ice cream. He told me he could not, would not *ever,* get enough of me. In quick succession, we got married and had a baby.

Nothing turns the illicit into the licit like settling down.

Was that the last party of my life, I wondered, as I surveyed the wreckage of my thirtieth birthday.

There'd been a pole on that bus. As my friends and I danced through the streets of Atlanta, banging like pinballs inside that great vehicle, eventually I got hold of that pole. My enthusiasm was clearly evident to onlookers: days later, I received an email from Lauren, one of my guests. I might enjoy the pole dance lessons she was taking at a local studio, she suggested. Within minutes of receiving her message, I signed up for a package. After I taught my classes at the university, I'd rush to the pole studio, my body hungry for bruises, my hips craving the bump and grind. It had been a long time since I'd felt like this. I had to admit, to feel this way again—alive, sexy, after hours lecturing in a blazer—felt like a return to a fire I'd extinguished in my own best interest, a woman I'd never stopped wanting. *Would* never stop wanting. I had denied that desire. Looked away from it. Wrote heady articles about complex literary theory to muffle the sounds of longing scratching at my door. I buried a woman in the basement of my heart. Sometimes, in the middle of the night, baby on my breast, I'd forgotten she existed, so deep in the earth was she.

The things we bury will grow.

As I'd practice my tricks on a pole I installed smack dab in the middle of the den of our small apartment, in the bedroom next door, my baby cried. I sent my husband after him with a pacifier and flipped myself upside down, milk streaming down my face.

One evening after pole class, Lauren approached me.

"Hey," she said, "I've just gotta ask. Have you ever been a stripper?"

"How'd you know?"

"Oh. It's very evident."

A thrill rushed through my veins that I had not felt in years.

"Would you like to strip again?" she smiled. "Because I could help you with that."

A week later, I sat alongside Lauren on a barstool at the Funtime Pleasure Palace.

The Funtime: a wood-paneled warehouse where naked ladies danced for truckers emptying beers and filling up ashtrays. Against the back wall, a bulldog of a bouncer guarded a row of doorways, each covered by a black curtain. A woman with a butterfly tattoo spread full across her ass, a wing on each cheek, lead a bearded man behind one of those curtains. This is VIP. This is where the money is made.

It had been states away, years ago, since I'd been in a place like this. *I could pay off our student loans*, I imagined telling my husband, manipulating his natural tendency towards responsibility to bend him to my wishes. But also: I could feel like a woman again. Like me again. Not just a mom. Not just a wife. Not just an academic.

But—who was I? I hardly knew.

In my twenties, the strip club had provided a field upon which I could weaponize my trauma. I'd gotten addicted to the glamour, the cash, bruises on my knees. I'd lost much in my life due to this addiction. I'd tried to fix myself, tried to go straight. Got all the degrees; wore all the blazers. Yet, the addiction remained.

But—I was past that part of my life now? Or so I thought? Or so my husband thought. How could we know my reformation had been merely a phase? I was as certain to turn back to black as summer was to winter; seasonal, predictable; I'd never been able to keep up respectability. By the time we married, however, I was nearly thirty—and then, of course, we had the baby— and so, I thought—well, the reformation is complete; it must be. There are no hoes past thirty, and certainly none with infants and PhDs. I'd call it naivety if it weren't deliberate ignorance.

Who was I, I wondered as I sat on that barstool, my gaze drifting across the bodies of women ten years my junior. One thing was for sure: the woman I was contemplating reinventing was certainly not the woman my husband had signed up for. Not who I'd advertised. We met in grad school. We were teachers. I'd traded the dog collar for plain black flats.

But—I hadn't lied about myself.

I'd only been mistaken.

At first, Daddy thought Buster was a good dog. He certainly was smart.

However, as the months wore on, Buster got bigger.

And as Buster got bigger, he grew unwieldly.

His tail smashed into Mama's vase, knocking it to the floor with a crack. His wide paws tracked mud into the house, no matter that he'd rang the doorbell to let himself in.

Tricks weren't enough to save him anymore, I worried, as Mama scrubbed away Buster's footprints with a frown.

"Act right," I whispered to him, as I placed the vase back on the shelf, turning it so the crack faced the wall.

Daddy had saved Buster from a mean fate. He had picked him up from the rain and darkness outside. At first, Daddy was enamored of Buster's wildness, a feral dog come in from the streets.

That would soon change.

Wildness is only loveable when it's not fucking up your house.

The next night, I convinced my husband to let me strip.

"Consider the student loans," I argued.

He wouldn't look at me, fumbling with a napkin instead, folding it smaller and smaller, creating order in this ritual. This napkin, he can control. This woman, however, this woman—

Dave never sought to tame me. Indeed, he hadn't thought it necessary. My degeneracy was evident upon our first meeting. Yet perhaps he assumed the tattoos and the cigarettes and the feral in my eyes lingered only as remnants of a life I'd left behind. He'd spent a lifetime among the thoroughly well-behaved. He came to Louisiana for something different. He left Louisiana with me. And here I was, wavering from the promises I'd insinuated. I removed my lip ring for our wedding. I purchased a wardrobe from the ladies' section in Macy's. I settled down and had his baby. All of these things, I'd designed. We think there will come a time when we are certain of our identity; we await a moment of arrival in which we have at last *become*. Yet I continued to become, looking ever further to whatever mystery awaited. I vowed to my husband that I would stay a certain way. I failed to keep that vow, and many others, as well.

When Dave is uncomfortable, he retreats within. An invisible barrier rises before him. I call it the glass wall. The glass wall rises, and the light in his eyes vanishes. It's as if he's hit a switch, turned himself off to me. *Hello in there*, I sing to him, waving my hands, trying to pull him out.

But sometimes, when it's convenient—

I leave him behind glass.

Things happen in a marriage: Mama always warned me of that. Anyone expecting the heat of wild love to continue past combustion was woefully misled. Be realistic. He won't chase you around the house forever. And—let's be fair—you won't always spill love letters onto the page through wine-drunk midnights. A baby comes, the privilege of romance gives way to sleepy-headed resentment over whose turn it is to change the diaper. When the world ripped us apart, my love, we grasped tenaciously to stay together. When the world pushed us together, my love, we turned away from one another in bed, your back against mine.

"Strip if you want to," he conceded. I chose not to wave my hands, chose not to say *hello in there*, chose to leave the wall between us, where he could not stand in my way.

There was no audition. The Funtime Pleasure Palace took me on sight. This would not be the case with other clubs.

"She wants to work," Lauren said, as we shivered in the parking lot behind the dressing room.

The house mom propped the back door open with her hip, standing in the crack between her world and ours, a battered clipboard in her hands. I looked over her shoulder into the dressing room: a tangle of nudity and noise, Caboodles and tattoos, cigarettes and flat irons aglow. The smell of AquaNet floated through the air, a flammable frenzy of sequins and big ideas.

The house mom took a drag off her Virginia Slim and eyed me up in an instant.

"This the one you brought in the other night?"

"Yep," Lauren replied.

"Well. She looks all right to me."

Mama handed me some forms, took my driver's license, and just like that, I had a job, and I never even had to take off my winter coat.

"So…when do I come in?" I asked Lauren as we left the parking lot.

"Doesn't matter."

"Well…what should I wear?"

"Doesn't matter."

"Doesn't *anything* matter?" I asked, and she laughed.

"Obviously not. Isn't that why you came?"

Customers generally regard activities that happen with a stripper as activities that don't count. In that dark closet, we become the fantasy that you don't have to acknowledge in the light. We are the dream you wake from and forget, something from another consciousness, another world. Something you are not responsible for.

I hope I can remember how to do this.

Lauren beckoned me to her table, where she entertained an old man with a skeletal face and an expensive suit. "This is Lux's first night here," she cooed in his ear, stroking a single nail up the papery skin of his wrist.

"Virgin territory," he said, licking his lips, a reservoir of spittle clinging white in the corner of his mouth, his gaze sliding over every part of me.

"Not exactly," I shot back.

I was no virgin. No novice. No kid. Sure, it had been a few years since I'd stripped, but I'd lost nothing in the interim—not the skills, nor the baggage, that drove me. No, I'd brought it all with me, these pieces of myself I'd thought I'd buried, sprouting toward the sun in spite. "No good stripper ever says retire," Sheena had told me, the night I quit the Styxx. I never gave her full credit for the wisdom she possessed.

"You should take Johnny to VIP," Lauren said, planting a dry kiss on his cheek. "He loves to slow dance."

"Is that true?" I asked Johnny. "You slow dance in VIP?"

"No," he responded. "I eat pussy in VIP."

The next morning, I couldn't sleep past eight. I hadn't gotten home until four, didn't crawl into bed until six, yet motherhood had programmed early mornings into my body. Even more disturbingly, I was worried about how my husband was going to react on my first morning-after. My eyes popped open with a jolt of fear.

"I made three-hundred and sixty dollars," I told him, as disheveled and aching I shuffled into the den, left-over lash glue catching one eye closed. Dave looked up from the floor where he stacked blocks with our son. The baby reached out to me, smiling bright to see his mommy. I scooped his chubby body into my arms.

"Oh," Dave replied, eyes trained on the blocks, balancing.

"That's a pretty good amount, don't you think?"

"I guess."

I searched his face, struggling to catch his eye. My heart sank with a familiar horror. Had I done it again?

Another man had loved me once, a love tender and wild and true. A man had opened himself to me, exposed his bare breast, and decided at last that he could not withstand my violence. And then, a gift from the heavens descended upon my wretched soul: Dave entered my life. Again, I'd felt that sweet fury, that magnet-pull between two unguarded hearts with everything to lose and only each other to gain. I'd spilled my guts into poetry through the dark nights of six solid weeks over Dave—only to push him away now? What self-destruction was this? And yet, Lux beckoned. And yet, she positioned herself upon a stage. Dazzling. Intoxicating. Impossible to say no.

"Are you…mad at me?" I ventured.

"Nope."

"You sure?"

"Yep."

"Maybe I could take us out to dinner tonight?"

"That's not necessary."

Silence hung between us. What was there to say? How was your night? He didn't want to know. Would never want to know. I couldn't blame him. I don't think I've ever had a man from whom I didn't have to hide.

"Hello in there…?" I offered.

He didn't look up.

As once-weekly Fridays turned into thrice-weekly shifts at the Funhouse, it wasn't unusual for me to leave the club with a grand or more any given night.

There are lines you draw in the beginning, things you said you would never do. Money—and everything that money signifies—moves those.

During daytimes I sifted through the humdrum task of looking for academic jobs—non-tenure-track "temporary" appointments with absurd workloads making up the majority of offerings. Even those gigs were swamped with impossible odds: hundreds of other newly-minted PhDs, fighting tooth and nail for degrading-ass appointments. Once I found an *unpaid* instructorship on the job list. Nope. I thought being an English professor meant I'd write poems in a wood paneled office, grade a few papers on the side. False. I finished my schooling at a time in which the academy was cranking out PhDs and sending them into a world with no jobs, certainly not fair ones, and the ones that you *could* get invariably meant moving somewhere far away, probably Bumfuck, to teach hundreds of bored students a composition course they were forced to take.

Shit. I didn't want that.

I'd come to love Atlanta. I'd made a family here. After three degrees and three states in the last decade, I was ready to settle down. I wasn't twenty anymore. Hell, I was thirty. I didn't want to pack up boxes and head for another temporary stint at another temporary home.

Once you realize that you can make a thousand dollars in a night, the knowledge dogs you. It slinks through your subconscious, starving, scratching at your door whenever shit gets tough. Or ambitions run high.

One can, after all, always go back to stripping.

I danced naked on tables the night I defended my dissertation.

CHAPTER NINE
WHIRLWIND OF DEPRAVITY

I developed a twitch in my head grading freshman essays. Across my skull, a muscle jumped like a plucked rubber band. As I poured over the stack of papers, I pressed a finger against my head to still the spasms. Nonetheless, beneath my touch, my body flexed beyond my command.

This was not what I had planned when I left Richmond for a life of the mind.

When I left Richmond, Louisiana-bound for grad school, visions of my own prolific artistry drove me. I dreamed no dreams of grading papers. Instead, I entertained romantic fantasies about what a scholarly life would mean—art and artists, books written, poems penned. And so I collected an MA and signed up for a PhD, packed my bags, and moved yet again.

Yet, on the first day of orientation at Georgia State, the department head informed us flatly, "There are no jobs for any of you." The moment I heard those words, an anxiety sank into my guts that didn't leave for years.

After my graduation, I'd accepted a postdoctoral fellowship teaching Freshman Comp at Georgia Tech, my sole academic offering among the dozens of applications I'd sent out. I didn't particularly want the gig. But I needed to be grateful for any crumbs thrown my way.

In order to achieve success in the academy, one need not merely excel. Instead, one must excel among an ocean of over-achievers driven by ambition for mastery of the most obscure topics imaginable. Who, her? She's an expert on the sense of smell in the works of William Faulkner. Him? He writes about assonance in the poetry of the transcendentalists.

It was no surprise that my scholarly focus turned to bad women. My favorite character was Edna Pontellier. When she swam out into that ocean, I swam with her. Disallowed. A woman you can't categorize.

I was navel-gazing through scholarship, lacking the courage to face myself straight on.

My short tenure at Funtime—which had also been my reintroduction to stripping at the geriatric age of thirty—had been a whirlwind of depravity, one I'd dived into quickly, a perfect storm of my darkest desires ignited like a match dropped into gasoline. The time I had spent during my break from stripping had marked the longest expanse of good behavior in my life—three degrees, a wedding, and a baby. That expanse had primed me to explode into vice.

I met Bob barside one evening, a few weeks into my employment. An unassuming guy in a button-up, Bob was middle-aged, quiet, and awkward. He patronized the Funtime at least once a week, a worried smile on his face while his eyes scanned everything in the room but you.

"I don't…relish eye contact," he admitted, early in our relationship.

I didn't have to beg with Bob. He was ready to spend. Unguarded in that back closet, drunk on my smile, the weight of my body in his lap, the movement of my thigh between his legs, all love and body and no demands—Bob would often get so worked up that he'd buy another session or three.

Some clubs keep their VIP sections closely surveilled. Others do not. The Funtime fell into the latter category. Both a boon and a burden, this lack of surveillance: the freedom to do whatever was necessary to make money, I appreciated. The liberties granted the customers, I feared.

At first, Bob only wanted the usual. Grinding, his name on my lips.

Until one day, he closed his hand over my throat, and I realized with a start what he truly desired.

My position at Tech had "temporary" in its title. My fellow postdocs pounded out research, pumped up their resumes, and headed committees in preparation for the return of application season. I couldn't conjure the interest to match their efforts, much less the drive. Therefore, a temporary was all I'd ever be.

Georgia Tech is a beautiful school adorned in wealth. Having taught in southern Louisiana where classrooms featured rat nests and actual holes in the walls, the pristine facilities at Tech had me convinced that I had somehow snuck in on a rich people's party. Entire walls consisted of whiteboard; intricate control panels sat atop the teaching podium, thousands of dollars' worth of gadgets available at my fingertips.

At new faculty orientation, white folks in seersucker suits and pearls chatted over delicate appetizers passed around on silver platters by the gloved hands of brown people. I looked uneasily at my colleague. "We shouldn't be doing this," I whispered, as I took another strawberry from a tray.

"Stop taking the fucking strawberries then," she hissed back.

I'd suspected I'd been living inauthentically for a while now.

Buster couldn't get enough of life. Mama and I gave him treats—Kraft singles, beef bones, even chicken from our plates—always sneaking him little yum-yums whenever Daddy wasn't looking—but these gifts were never enough. Buster wanted what he could not have. And so, he chased down the neighbor's cat, ran squirrels up the trees, sniffed at my lunchbox when I headed out for school.

On rare occasions, Mama would make Daddy a special cake. Pineapple upside down cake, a time-consuming recipe, Daddy's favorite. Perhaps the commitment, the care, made that cake so sweet to him. Mama didn't make it often. She was mad at Daddy a lot. But one day, Mama got to baking. While Daddy slept, tired from another graveyard shift, his wife did for him something kind.

"Being married ain't one big long date," Mama often told me, growing up. When Daddy stole Mama from her first husband, he promised her she'd never sit through another man's meanness again. He promised to cherish her. He squeezed her waist and told her he loved her littleness. And then, Mama gained weight—and an attitude. Daddy's tiny smiling baby turned into his unsatisfied wife. Whereas before she'd been a fountain of sweetness, years of marriage and raising children had turned her into a well of complaints.

Daddy signed up for another year on the third shift.

A woman wants to be held at night. Yet my mama went that whole marriage sleeping alone. During the scant hours while Daddy wasn't at work or asleep, he spent his time in his workshop, painting, or putting together an engine for another lawnmower we did not need. Well before he died, Daddy was gone. Growing up, family felt mostly like Mama and me. My brothers had friends, sports, teenage lovers. Daddy had work, and his art. Mama and I had each other.

Mama didn't like people in her kitchen, but on the day of the pineapple upside down cake, she allowed me to help. As we folded the wet ingredients into the dry, she told me about their wedding day, how they eloped, how their celebration dinner consisted of a couple of burgers from a drive-in joint, their honeymoon a flea-bag motel at the top of a hill. She'd been divorced from Steve nary a month, but so wildly in love were my future parents, they couldn't wait any respectable amount of time to dedicate their lives to one another. "Every marriage needs a passionate beginning," Mama always said, "because it sure as shit don't get easier."

In the early days of my motherhood, hello and goodbye were the same in my family. Dave would walk in the door, and I'd hand him the baby and walk out, his workday ending just as mine began.

One evening, Dave came home looking green. He stumbled into our home, groaned, then vomited half his body weight into the trash can. Trembling, he crawled into bed.

How could he do this to me?

"You can't watch the baby?" I asked, frantic. "This is only my second class of the semester! I'm going to look awful if I cancel!"

Ashen, he buried himself deeper into the sheets.

"Looks like you're coming with me tonight," I said to our son.

I shoved my computer into my bookbag, concocting plans A, B, and C for how to handle this situation. Too late for a sitter.

Too late even for a cancellation email. I certainly couldn't *not* show up. Yet, what impression would I make on these students, baby feet dangling from a sling across my chest as I stood before them and broke down the structure of an argumentative essay?

"I'm cold," Dave whispered from the bed, wadding a quilt beneath his chin, his face beaded with sweat. I touched his head. Burning up.

"There's not enough blankets in the world to keep you warm," I spat, ripping the covers from his grasp and chucking them into a pile of dirty laundry as the baby and I headed out the door.

Shifts at the Funtime ended at four in the morning. After years living within the nine-to-five schedule of the civilized world, staying up this late tasted sweetly of youth.

"Waffle House?" Lauren would suggest at the end of each shift, and at the end of each shift, I would accept. Starving, feeling due that fistful of heart-clogging deliciousness, she and I never missed a middle-of-the-night bacon-egg-and-cheese feast.

"I'll have the usual," I told the waitress, absently. My thoughts were elsewhere, tangled and fretful. That night, things had gone too far with Bob. What's worse—we'd gotten caught. I panicked in silence, too embarrassed to share my situation with Lauren or anyone else. Would I lose my job? There's all kinds of shit going on in those back rooms—certainly they wouldn't single me out? Butterfly-Ass gave more head than a pilsner. And the Barbie twins? They blasted coke from eight p.m. until dawn, jabbering like toddlers. As Lauren placed her order, I comforted myself with other women's crimes, ranking them in my mind as worse than my own. Sure, the bouncer had walked in on me in a compromising position. But rules didn't matter at the Funtime, right?

"Two bacon-egg-and-cheese sandwiches," the waitress confirmed. "Got it."

My eyes followed her as she walked back to the counter with our order. She's cute, I thought. Why does she work at the diner for pennies when the Funtime is only steps away?

"She ought to come next door," I told Lauren. "The money's over there."

"The money's not there for *me*."

"You didn't have a good night?"

"No," Lauren replied, picking at her nails.

"Oh."

"I know *you* did, though," she said, looking up. "You were in the back all night with that guy."

"You must be rich," I had remarked to Bob once, as he ordered another session.

"No," he replied, "just totally irresponsible."

"So what's he like," Lauren asked. "Is he easy?"

He'd started out easy enough.

A hand on the throat, and then a tremble, and then goodbye.

The next time: a hand on the throat again, but this time, tighter.

Is this what we do, I wondered on his third visit of this nature, collecting three sessions of VIP fare from his trembling palm. It was. The next time he came to me, he asked if we could stand instead of sit. I agreed. In response, he pinned me to the wall. At least he isn't invading my body, I rationalized; his mild violence seemed worth the seven hundred he'd blow in these fits of insanity. I felt nothing but the shame.

"Is this okay," he whispered, gripping me tighter. I nodded, in spite of myself. Maybe this man might like to kill women? What void does he fill here now, with me? Why does he search for an appropriate receptacle for his violence? Why have I agreed?

I was somebody's mother. Somebody's wife. A doctor.

"He's easy enough," I told Lauren.

"Sure wish I could get one like him."

I shudder to confess, even now, the things I've done. I have kept myself hidden from those who love me in order to maintain the freedom to do what I want. I've adopted fake names, donned fake hair, conjured within my heart a brand-new woman each night, separating myself even from myself, to maintain the detachment necessary for me to enact my dark scenes.

The crimes I have committed would be unforgiveable to many. Perhaps I am included among that number.

Why did I make those choices; why did I say yes when I should say no? I hardly knew. Money? As long as I left my mind unexamined, I could pretend it was about money. "Burying it in sand," my husband calls it—the practice of repressing uncomfortable thoughts and feelings. It is an art he has perfected.

"How do you feel about me stripping?" I'd ask him, from time to time.

"I don't," he'd answer.

In sand, our pain seems silent. It isn't, of course. It screams, scratches at the mass above, clawing its way through the earth with the dogged determination of the ignored.

From the counter, the pineapple-upside-down cake beckoned Buster. Sweetness, dripping in butter and sugar. One bite, one lick, one taste—that would be enough.

And so, he sprung.

And so, he leapt at the counter, higher than him, the cake just out of reach.

Pounding at the countertop in reckless hunger, his hurried scramble only slid the cake farther away. And so, he took what he'd learned outside, and stood on his hind legs, reached his front paw out gingerly, just as he'd done to ring the doorbell. In this way, he made contact with the cake, slid it closer to the edge. There was an art to getting what you were not allowed to have. One lick, one taste, would be enough.

Of course, it wasn't.

By the time Mama found him, he was sticky and wasted, the cake in hunks on the ground. Soon, he would be sick from all of this. But not now. Not yet.

"Oh no," Mama moaned.

"What will we do?" I asked, panicked. Daddy didn't get a lot of nice things. Daddy worked all the time.

"Your father will be furious," Mama said, eyebrows knotted as she surveyed the wreckage smeared across her kitchen.

"Can you make another?"

Buster shone his happy face upon me, tail thudding against the floor.

"There isn't time...."

"We've got to hide this," I said, wringing my little hands. Daddy got mad sometimes. Especially at Mama.

"You used to love me. You used to adore me," I'd overheard her say to him, one early morning as he entered their bed just as she exited.

"Yes," she agreed. "Let's get to work."

And that's when we heard Daddy's footsteps in the hall.

"Shit's not as good as it seems," I told Lauren.

The waitress clunked our plates down in front of us.

"Bacon-egg-and-cheese?" she asked, sucking her tooth, scanning our faces.

"That's right," Lauren replied.

"Y'all been out tonight?"

"Why do you ask?"

"Well, because most people that come in here this late been out. And y'all come in here late quite a bit."

"I think you know where we've been," Lauren answered.

"Oh!" said the waitress. She cocked her head and smiled, challenged. Lauren was speaking rudely to her, and she didn't have to stand for it. "I reckon I *do* know where y'all been!" She scowled and turned on her heel.

"Look at her," I said to Lauren, watching the waitress swish her ass from side to side clear across that diner. "I told you she could do well at the Funhouse."

"'Least one of us could," Lauren remarked. She removed a single sweet pickle slice from her sandwich, bit it between her front teeth. She glared at me. "Not all of us get money just handed to us," she said.

"What do you think Bob is paying for," I asked, staring right back.

"Oh. I've got my theories."

I looked to my plate. Grease gleamed under the fluorescent light. This was one staring contest I'd lost.

Few things are more demanding of one's social graces than convincing strangers to pay to see you naked. Bob's continued patronage eased some of that burden for me.

Nonetheless, working for Bob created its own demands.

He was panting, out of his mind, by the time the bouncer discovered our evil arrangement.

Certainly, Bob had a fetish for violence. Yet in other ways, he was meek. The things he enjoyed, he did not expect for free, nor without consent—and he never indulged without a measure of embarrassment. Barside, balding and quiet, Bob was the epitome of an average guy: clean and nervous, harboring weird desires that drove him to strange places in the night. Might be a serial killer; might just need a friend. Spin the wheel.

What had begun as another nearly-identical engagement with a customer—small talk and grinding—had evolved, visit by visit, into sadism. The build-up from me bouncing on his lap to him choking me against the wall was so gradual I barely registered it. I suppose I was numb to violence from men, had understood it viscerally as a woman's lot in life, a rite of passage one simply goes through, sometimes more than once, and something you might as well get paid for if you could withstand it.

They say you'll repeat a mistake until you learn the lesson.

I didn't know how I let it come to this. I would never have agreed to such a scenario had it been the initial proposition. Excuses I could make for myself include: my warped youth had left an indelible mark on my adult behavior; the money coerced me; everybody else was doing it. Each of these reasons has merit. But—I wasn't a kid anymore. I wasn't a neglected miscreant wondering the trailer park.

I was a grown-up.

I knew better.

Knowledge, I never lacked.

It was morality that was missing.

"I wish I had a Bob," Lauren often said.

Lauren, you don't want a Bob. What I was earning in cash, I was paying for with live recreations of ancient wounds. Here, in this closet, I accepted fistfuls of twenties in exchange for abuse. I was the kind of woman who took payment for abuse. Used to it, trained to accept it, normalize it. Lauren thought Bob was easy. I couldn't tell her, couldn't tell anybody, the price I was paying for his money.

It was at the end of another of these sadistic sessions when the bouncer walked in.

"What the fuck do you call this?" he demanded.

Bob dropped me from his grip.

"Get out," the bouncer growled.

Bob fled, red-faced and sweating, without glancing once my way.

"Not you," the bouncer spat, as I tried to slide past in similar fashion. "What's your name?"

"Lux."

He scribbled on his clipboard.

"We were just talking—"

"Sure ya were. Get the fuck out of here."

Afterwards, I smoked cigarettes at the bar, shaking with fear, awaiting a summons to the manager's office. However, the call never came.

Perhaps—I would get away with this?

Perhaps not.

"What the hell happened?" Daddy asked, eyes scanning the kitchen floor, smeared in streaks of yellow and white.

Mama took my hand.

"Buster got to the cake," she answered.

"Please, Daddy, please! Don't be mad!"

"What cake?"

"I…made you a cake today. I can make you another—"

Daddy frowned. Hunks of sweetness, fashioned by my mother's hand, sprawled ruined across the floor. Icing smeared on the counter, down the cabinets, ground into the gap between the doors. In the corner, a single pineapple ring told the tale of what goodness had once been. Daddy's eyes lit on that ring.

Just then, Buster approached him, panting happy and tail wagging, sugar glazed across his nose.

And Daddy—kicked him.

The yelp from that dog struck me in my guts.

"Daddy, don't!"

I pulled at his shirt as he cranked up for another blow. Then a grunt, a kick, screams—mine, the dog's, Mama's. As he raged through our home, shouting curses and damning Buster, I collected my dog and hid in the corner, scooping him onto my lap, lugging his heavy weight upon mine into a rocking chair.

I wrapped my arms around Buster's warm body, felt him tremble as Daddy slung a row of books from the shelf. I knew it was over for us. My love would be severed, taken away. A switch had been flipped in my Daddy.

"A man can only take so much," he hollered, as inside the kitchen, my mama scrubbed and cried.

The love between Dave and me began as a secret. In that secrecy, we shared everything. There was nothing to lose by baring it all. We were officially nothing, after all. Watching Dave walk out of my door in Louisiana, I spilled my guts, no pretense. Choose me, I pleaded. He responded honestly, as well: he could not choose me. And with these truths, we covered each other in kisses and tears, books in boxes our companions on the floor.

After the pain, the joy: "I am leaving her because my love for you is too great to stay." To see his face again at the door of that Red Roof Inn in Richmond, Virginia—joy as I had never known. He left the life he was supposed to lead. He broke every rule for me.

I was used to losing. Used to goodbye. Rejection, I understood. And yet, Dave came back to me. And then—he stayed. All that had been forbidden—became suddenly allowed. We treasured one another for years.

And then, small crimes. I jerked the blanket from him when he was sick. He'd come home from work and put his head directly back into it, disappearing from me in the day, and then disappearing again in the night. I painted my face and sought affection from other men, did crazy shit in closets. He didn't notice. He didn't ask. He buried himself in sand against me. Small crimes, bricks we laid in the construction of us.

When I felt myself slipping, becoming too awful, I tried to buy back his love. In the early days, when cash was short, I used the currency of my body to atone for my sins. But by the time I was stripping, I had actual money to spend. He hated cleaning the house. I hired a house cleaner. He loved the beach. I took him to the beach. He needed a new car. We bought him a new car. Apologizing with gifts, purchasing permission. Spending cash to save myself.

"Breakfast on you?" Lauren suggested as we stood at the register. This would be our last meal together, though we didn't know that yet. She was joking, but I paid anyway.

As I was getting in my car, she stopped me.

"One question," she asked.

"Yeah?"

"You ever end up dancing for that old guy, Johnny?"

"Sure. A time or two."

"Did he ever—try it with you?"

"Try what?"

"You know."

"I don't."

I did.

He had.

She smiled.

"You're not scared of anything, are you?" she asked.

"I'm scared to death."

I'm a girl who breaks the rules. She is a rule-follower. Between her kind and mine, there resides an old contempt. Lauren had introduced me to the Funtime; she'd been the permission-giver. I owed her at least honesty. Kindness. Yet, I could conjure neither. Our unspoken competition had gained us nothing but dollars and dissolved affections.

"I miss you," Lauren would text me, a few weeks later, after I'd moved on to bigger and better things.

I missed her too. I missed catching her face across the crowd, a smile from the stage, the promise of breakfast and a friend at the end of a long night. She was one good thing at the Funtime. Maybe I'd been the same for her? I missed her—that was the truth.

And that's what I should've texted her back.

Instead, I left her on read.

CHAPTER TEN
Top Shelf Anything

"This ain't working out," the bouncer said, and spit on the ground.

"Why?" I asked—but I knew.

As I lugged my bag through the parking lot, the devastating gravity of the situation hit me: just months after becoming a doctor, I had been fired from a ramshackle titty bar on the outskirts of town.

"I think I've reached rock bottom," I told my husband when I arrived home.

"Did you ever hear back from that Clayton State position?" he replied.

"No."

"Well, keep waiting. That's probably better work for you."

A temporary employee must remember her status and behave accordingly. From the beginning of my post-doc at Tech, the goal was to find a real job. A job without "temporary" in the title.

Three English degrees had turned me myopic. The culture of the academy encourages this singular vision. There are no professional options discussed outside of the Ivory Tower. If one earns a PhD, one simply—becomes a professor. To fail in this regard meant a general failure at life.

Yet, the dissection of high literature for publication in obscure journals felt both irrelevant and misguided. How had I gotten this deep, travelled this doggedly off track? Who was I to dissect Faulkner all day? I wanted to be the writer, not the dissector. I languished behind a desk in an office without windows, crossing fingers and chanting incantations in hopes that a real life with real meaning would reveal itself to me sometime between grading essays.

"These positions pay half what I was making at Funtime," I told Dave, as I scoured job offerings.

"Well, you got all those degrees," he replied. "Might as well use them."

Dave never asked why Funtime fired me. Was he naïve, or just turning a blind eye? Either way, I'd take it. Yet while I appreciated the freedom his lack of concern provided, at the same time a certain resentment filled my heart: *my husband doesn't care about me.* At night, he obsessed over lesson plans while I applied false eyelashes in order to look pretty for other men. Maybe I didn't care about him, either? As I transformed myself into a new woman each weekend and walked out the door, I didn't recognize my own leaving. I only saw his: a quiet retreat, head-down in grammar worksheets at 10 p.m. on a Tuesday, while I longed for him to kiss my neck as he had in the bayou.

In the days following Buster's crime, Daddy grew distant, and I got sadder and sadder. I could sense the loss impending, knew my friend would be taken. And so I began to bring the dog to sleep with me, an indulgence previously not allowed and now conveniently ignored by the only parent home during bedtime. Mama pretended not to notice each night as I sobbed, clutching

Buster against my body, fingering that sixth toe, rubbing that smart knot, my bed filthy with fur. In the mornings, I would take him outside to practice his tricks, hoping to make him loveable for his inevitable new home. "Wherever you go," I whispered, Kraft single in hand, "please be good."

He tried to please us with tricks. He shook hands, rang the doorbell, sat on command. But he was, after all, an unwanted dog dropped off in the rain. He had urges he could not resist. And for these urges, he would be punished.

Calm down, Lindsay. Stop wracking this bed with your sobs. Enjoy these last days with your dog. You are, after all, only a little girl. Children shouldn't hurt so. A reel of good times spun behind my eyes: the wet puppy in Daddy's arms, the sound of the doorbell, Mama so pleased with her cake. We rolled through the grass on those last days, Buster and I, a rope bone in my hand, Buster barking cheerfully, tongue hung out in unknowing joy, no clue that these lessons would be our last.

Dogs don't know about "last." They don't know about goodbye. Why couldn't I be more like Buster, alive in this moment, enjoying our time together instead of grieving for its end?

I'd never been fired from any job, much less a strip club—and there was something particularly ignoble about being fired from Funtime. One had to fuck up fairly royally to get canned at this joint. I'd seen a dancer discovered with meth maintain her position. We'd all heard the moans coming from VIP, especially from the Barbie twins. Even management ran rampant with illegalities. As for me, I'd only been caught in one compromising position. My immediate expulsion seemed overkill.

Perhaps I had committed an even greater crime than being caught with a man's hands on me.

Perhaps—

I had descended into geriatric unattractiveness.

After I got fired, I had a dream. In that liminal space between sleep and waking, the delirious mid-consciousness of the anxiety-driven insomniac, I dreamed that I walked into the plastic surgeon's office, pointed at my lined forehead, my tired eyes, my falling face, and told him, "just fuck me up."

Back at Tech, I showed my students a black and white photo of me as a twenty-something punk rocker, an effort to relate to their youth, to earn their esteem. Earnestly, one of them asked, "Did they not have color photos back then?"

My darling child, would you also like to know what Jesus wrote in my yearbook?

The months I'd worked at the Funtime had doubled my once-meager income. Things that had once been desires, now became needs. I needed to write, so I hired a babysitter. I needed to sleep late, so I assuaged my husband's resentment with gifts while I snoozed away my half of the parenting. Perhaps I'd produce a nice homecooked dinner of pork chops and mashed potatoes later, try at least to act like a wife?

Like most lovers, Dave and I started hot, and then grew lukewarm. Over the years, that intent gaze he laid upon me in Louisiana, his listening ear, relaxed into a familial blind comfort: I walk into the room, and you don't see me. I tell a story, and at the end you look up, confused: have I been talking? Comfortable. Distracted. No fighting. What was there to fight over? We'd signed the papers. Had the child. Our fates were sealed. As he relaxed into benign absence, I took advantage of his disinterest to do whatever the fuck I wanted.

All I'd ever *really* wanted was a man to choose me. Dave had done that. He'd had the proper course laid before him, and he'd walked out that door and into mine. I had cast spells with my body and my words to manifest this reality. I was now living the dream. His addiction to me grew into commitment. His commitment settled; he is a man who loves order. He will never leave. I worked blood magic to earn this level of loyalty. And yet I longed still to be lit on fire. Longed for a man's hunger. I couldn't live and die without a man lifting his head as I walked by. I wanted to feel seen. Wanted. Prized. And so, as soon as I'd established exactly the life I'd engineered, I sought to tear it asunder with reckless indulgence of the heat I could not contain.

I lasted two weeks without a stripping gig before I was on the hunt for another.

This time, I wouldn't require Lauren as a guide. Indeed, I'd never needed her at all. My gifts had never been lost—they pumped forever through my veins. This time, I wouldn't need a friend. It was every woman for herself on the strip club floor; no need to pretend otherwise. No amount of after-hours Waffle House dates could erase the competition that lurked beneath the surface. In a house of mirrors in which one's standing rested on one's ability to separate men from cash, and one's ability to separate men from cash rested upon one's feminine charm, jealousy and distrust among dancers proved inevitable. Whatever club I ended up at next, I wouldn't attempt to transcend this natural order.

Where would I go? Atlanta certainly had no lack of options. The city boasted a strip club on every corner.

But—who would hire an old stripper?

Was I an old stripper?

I was determined to find out.

I sewed rhinestones onto a lace bra and painted my face with the artful care of a veteran hoe. "Be my friend now," I told the woman in the mirror. "I'm going to be *your* friend now," I promised her, even though we both knew our relationship has been tumultuous in the past.

"Do you think they'll hire me?" I asked my husband.

"Here's hoping."

Dave had become accustomed to the house cleaner, as well.

"The next time you see me," I told him, "I'll be a top-shelf stripper."

I slid a fur along my shoulders, silk hosiery up my thighs, and drove to the Esquire. It was rumored that Playmates and Penthouse Pets worked here.

I would test my worth among them.

Marble counters and crystal chandeliers greeted me upon arrival. *You'll spend money here*, the lobby informed customers, in all its grandeur. *You'll make money here*, that same grandeur promised me.

"I'm here to audition," I told the lady at the front desk.

A few moments later, a woman in a suit emerged from the back of the house.

"I'm Housemom Kelly," she said, smoothing the wrinkles in her pencil skirt. "I need you to undress."

Kelly donned the neat chignon, neutral lipstick, and buttoned-up blouse of a businesswoman. She inhabited a different dimension than we sex clowns, clad in false lashes and fake diamonds. Kelly was not a woman of the night. Kelly merely managed women of the night.

I followed Housemom Kelly through a labyrinth of weaving hallways to the dressing room in the back, where I discovered luxuries untold. Never in my stripper life had I seen such cleanliness, such beauty! What splendorous Oz had I entered? The dressing rooms I'd known before were menageries of refuse—chairs with hole spilling stuffing, mirrors with cracks, neon carpet scraps cobbled together in an unholy coat of many colors: strippers got the junk the house no longer wanted. This dressing room, however, was bright, fresh, new. "Eighty dancers are working tonight," Kelly informed me, but you'd never know it—the make-up counters spread out in generous rows, turning the room into a city of its own. With space for everyone to breathe, no one antagonized each other. Luxury enables peace. "Back here is our salon," Kelly told me as she led me even deeper, pointing to a room where a stylist and a make-up artist prepared two dancers for the night shift. "And there is our sun room," she continued, opening another door to reveal a tanning bed. Where are the overflowing ashtrays, I wondered; where is the hollering teenager breaking up with her boyfriend over the phone?

"Do you like what you see?" Kelly asked me.

These nice things. Mirrors lined with big round bulbs: movie-star mirrors. Women all blonde locks and rib-bones and implants, rhinestones and rich daddies. These women didn't cuss. These women had graced centerfolds. These women were high-class. And I stood to be among them. A Prada bag sat unattended on the counter next to a bundle of human hair. These nice things, existing casually in this place. I wanted to exist casually among them. Be a nice thing, too.

"It's beautiful," I replied.

"Take off your clothes," she requested.

Under Kelly's watchful eye, I undressed. As she inspected my body, circling me to check for dents, I stared stoically into the distance. Some of the dancers took a break from their preparations to observe. My heart pounded—what if I failed this test? What if Kelly deemed me too old, too ugly, to occupy her stable? The academic rejections, I could handle. I could not, however, handle a judgment ranking my beauty deficient. A *no* here would break my heart.

"You're too pale," Kelly concluded, "but that, we can fix. Put your outfit back on and follow me. You'll have to dance for the manager."

Panicked graduate students and newly-minted PhDs provided the cheapest labor in the academy, desperate for any work in a dry market. In the interest of taking advantage of this, the academy at large pumped out more PhDs than there were jobs. I was a product of this moment in history. In this terrifying professional wasteland, grown adults with doctorates celebrated low-paying temporary gigs in the middle of nowhere, and I became conditioned to rate my worth pretty low. Just get a job, I told myself, any job, anywhere, for any insulting compensation, and consider yourself lucky. The majority of my professional peers wouldn't even get that far. The majority would adjunct—the ultimate temporary gig—paid by the course, no office, no benefits, the measliest of wages.

Excel in this cruel professional gauntlet, and perhaps you will achieve excellence in your field: win awards, land publications, get tenure, the ultimate permanent position. However, mere excellence guaranteed nothing. Intimidating odds and unfair advantages waited on the other side of every job application: the son of a friend of the dean got the position, sorry. I begged recommendation letters from the greatest scholars I could corner at a conference: it's all about who you know.

What was meaningful work? I hardly knew. I knew that writing esoteric articles for a small readership of graduate students who were only reading my article in order to write their own amounted to little more than a self-perpetuating cycle of insular knowledge that the rest of the world didn't care about. What was meaningful work? I hardly knew. But I knew this intellectual circle jerk wasn't it.

But I was in deep, and didn't see a way out.

Program administrators at Georgia Tech encouraged us to create syllabi based upon our scholarship. I entitled my course "Unruly Women and the Politics of Representation." When I announced this course title in one of our meetings, my colleagues chuckled.

"The student body here will certainly find that topic… refreshing," a third-year fellow said to me during a break.

"What's that supposed to mean?"

"You'll find out."

"Kansas," my colleague told me, as we crossed campus after class. "Can't remember which city. Never heard of it."

"Kansas?"

"Only for a year. Then I'll hit the market again."

"Hit the market *again?*"

"Well, this is only a one-year appointment."

I couldn't.

Wouldn't.

"I am not leaving Atlanta," I told my husband when I got home. "Ever."

"Well, how many universities are local?"

"I saw a Strayer University in the mall. I'll teach at the goddamn mall."

"Could be worse."

"*What* could possibly be worse?"

I'd sent an application to Clayton State, the single local school offering a position for the next year. I use the word "local" loosely—campus was over an hour away—yet I'd become so numbed to the grotesque relocation opportunities presented to desperate applicants that an hour commute didn't faze me.

"We'd like to bring you in for an interview," they finally replied.

An interview? Few applicants ever made it this far!

"I must be one of only three, maybe four, people up for this job," I told my husband.

"That's exciting!"

"Yes," I agreed, knowing full well that I did not want this job, nor any job like it. Yet I'd invested so much. Three degrees. Over a decade of dedication. How long could a person pretend, I wondered? Her whole life?

"You'd have a few long days," the head of the hiring committee informed me, as we volleyed emails. "Monday, Wednesday, Friday would start with eight a.m. classes and end with seven p.m. classes. You wouldn't be done until nine thirty at night…"

"I can handle long days."

Kelly led me onto the club's main floor. Where were the truckers, the scowling bouncers, the managers blasting bullets of cocaine? Where were the duct-taped bar stools, the makeshift pole fashioned in Tanya's uncle's basement?

In place of the accoutrement to which I had become accustomed, I found instead: leather couches. Marble bars. Bouncers with kind eyes? A replica of Venus de Milo posed under museum lights? A four-star restaurant flanked the main stage. At tables, important men held important meetings over fifty-dollar steaks. Dancers lined up by the dozens along a great catwalk, blending among the smoke and lights into an undulating landscape of round breasts and thigh gaps. At their feet gathered gentleman who may or may not be gentleman, but looked very, very rich.

"Well, go on ahead," encouraged Kelly, nudging me toward the catwalk.

I scaled the stairs to take my place on stage. Somewhere out there, among the leather and the marble and the gentlemen who may or may not be gentlemen, somewhere among those shadows, stood a manager, poised to rank me against the thousands of women he'd ranked before.

I did not have big breasts. I did not have long hair. My ribs could not be counted. In these arenas, I was deficient. I did, however, possess experience—half a lifetime's worth.

I caught the attention of a customer. Holding his gaze, I unfastened my garter, rolling the stocking down. A mirror ball spun above me, scattering luminescence across my body. I blinked slowly, languidly, holding his gaze like a milk-drunk baby. I ran my hands where I wanted his eyes to travel, and he followed my lead. Over my breasts, across my belly, resting for a moment at the triangle between my thighs, his gaze followed, only to return again and again to my eyes. *Yes*, I whispered. *Yes.*

He nodded slowly and reached for his wallet.

"You're different," he told me, placing a twenty in my garter.

"You're hired," Kelly said.

I did not get the job at Clayton State.

I purchased a two-hundred-dollar suit for the interview. It hangs still in my closet: a grey blazer and knee-length pencil skirt, an outfit one could only describe as "handsome." I drove an hour to campus, wondering all the while—add this drive to long workdays advertised, and when will I ever see my child? My husband? What would be the consequences of this absenteeism? Better not to think about. There were no other options that I could discern. Obviously, I could not strip forever. Obviously, I had to get a real life.

For the first part of the interview, I toured the campus alongside a jovial man, a future colleague should the interview go well. A casual walk with casual conversation was the pretense. Perhaps a decade my senior and just the kind of man I knew how to charm, intellectually sophisticated and quick to laughter, he smiled by my side. As we strolled together along the green hills of that county school, my heels clicking against the sidewalk, we were almost having fun. I smiled at all the right times. He made clever remarks and I acknowledged them. Things looked good.

For the second portion of the interview, I sat at a table across from a woman. She also appeared to be a decade my senior. Immediately, I sensed hostility. As she shot me probing questions about literary theories that in all honesty did not interest me, an energy of disapproval buzzed beneath her inquisitions. Whereas the man had wanted me to giggle, the woman wanted me to falter.

"Your thoughts on reader-response theory?" she asked.

"There is no objective truth outside of the reader's experience…?"

She balked.

"You don't really believe that, do you?"

I awoke one morning to find Buster missing from my bed.

I rushed into the kitchen, where I found Daddy.

"Where is he?" I cried.

"Gone."

"Gone?"

"Gone."

Eyes trained on his coffee, Daddy explained that Buster had moved to a farm where he could run around, be free. A big wide field would be better for Buster, better for everyone. The dog had gotten unwieldy. "He needs freedom," Daddy explained.

"What he needs is a friend!"

For years to come, I would believe that story: the farm, and the wide field, my dog running laps. Maybe Buster found a home big enough to hold him, a place that wasn't full of breakable things, a kitchen not laden with the delicious smells of cake he could not have. Maybe he wasn't once again dropped off in the rain. Maybe he'd found another child to feed him Kraft singles, another little girl stronger than me, strong enough to keep him, strong enough to not let them take him away. No more getting into trouble for you, Buster; no more demands to obey.

However, as years passed and I grew wiser, I began to doubt the truth of Daddy's story. Who did we know that owned a farm?

I cycled out the fishnets I'd worn at the Funtime, and in their place purchased the floor-length black evening gown required by the Esquire.

Each night at eleven, all dancers were required to drop whatever they were doing, no matter how lucrative, and report to the dressing room to prepare for "Walk Out," a pageant designed to hock lap dances at the discounted rate of five dollars a pop. En masse backstage, dancers donned black gowns and formed a single-file line, each woman waiting to ascend the catwalk. One by one, the DJ would announce each dancer, and she would promenade the catwalk to join the others in a line-up, a spectacle of grown adults in prom gowns.

Once all of the ladies had lined up, Walk Out culminated in the Two-for-One Special. At the encouragement of the DJ— "this is pay-per-view, not Cinemax!"—customers approached the catwalk, cash in hand, to select their favorite from the array. Those dancers selected receive the dubious honor of giving two demoralizingly-cheap lap dances. However, great woe and sorrow to those left lingering on stage, ignored and unchosen, forced to sway through two songs of shame for an audience that's not interested in them at all.

Unlike any other club I've ever worked at, The Esquire provided new girls with a detailed orientation and tour.

However, they forgot to tell me one thing:

Watch out for that stair on the catwalk.

Evening gown flowing, jewels sparkling, a spray tan disguising the unacceptable pallor of my actual complexion, I entered my first Walk Out line-up confident—a top-shelf stripper.

"Introducing Lux!" the DJ boomed.

I took a deep breath and parted the curtain, prepared to glide across that catwalk and into the hearts of every man in that joint. I bestowed a smile upon my audience as I lifted my foot to take the first step.

And then—

My legs flew over my head. My arms flailed. Onto my back I dropped with a thunderous clap, the weight of my body turning the stage into a bellowing drum. As I struck the floor, air expelled from my lungs with a grunt. Pain surged through my chest. The club erupted—exploded—ignited in laughter. *I missed the step. My god, there was a step there, and I missed it.* I struggled to stand, to breathe, to smile, to appear as if this didn't bother me at all.

Of course, it was no surprise when, as the laughter died down and customers crowded the catwalk to make their Two-for-One selections, I alone remained standing, the single ignoble unchosen.

"You're different!" the customer had told me at audition—and boy, was he right.

Who was I fooling?

I'd never be a top-shelf anything.

CHAPTER ELEVEN
RELAX INTO THE INSANITY

Let me tell you about Krystal.

Nothing about her is fair.

Big lips, big tits, tiny waist, long nails: bought and paid for, the lot of it. "I don't look a damn thing like I used to," she told me once, laughing: the woman is fully self-aware. Through starving and carving, she had achieved feminine perfection, beauty of a fragile sort. She'd fostered that fragility, nurtured it with self-denial and needles in the face, created herself in the image of a god we both know well.

I hated her for it.

As I watched her walk bored across the stage, no attempt at dancing, it dawned on me—all Krystal has to do is exist in this flawless body, and she is rewarded. Hordes of men flocked to her. Where was the justice? I was jealous. How could we occupy the same battleground in any fairness when she had purchased the necessary goods to achieve perfection, and I in my righteousness would never stoop so low? I'd clip fake hair into my head, sure. I'd glue fake hair on my eyelids. I'd paint my face every color of the rainbow. I'd slice stinging cuts a millimeter from my asshole trying to shave the most minute of offending hairs. But plastic surgery? No. I drew the line there.

That line, you see, secured my moral superiority.

Kept me "real" while she was "fake."

My beauty might not be as good as hers, but at least I'd come by it honestly, I told myself, as I coated my lips in a serum made of bee venom in order to make them swell.

I was thinking thusly upon her when I felt her hand on my shoulder.

"I saw you fall on stage the other night," she said.

"Utterly. Humiliating."

We perched at the high top next to the dressing room, surveying the crowd. She pulled out a cigarette, held it between her manicured fingers. "I should quit this shit," she remarked as she lit up, and I nodded in agreement, then lit mine too.

"How long have you been dancing?" she asked.

"A lifetime."

"I figured."

"How?"

"Well, you're not exactly nineteen, no offense. But then again, neither am I."

"You look nineteen."

"Far from it," she replied. "I'm way too old for this shit."

"I was *born* too old for this shit."

"I did a VIP on Friday, and that bastard bit me! And you know what? It barely even bothered me." She knocked the ash of her cigarette hard, laughed. "And that—*that's* what bothers me."

"In a way, it's a gift, the numbness."

"Puking has become part of my routine," she continued. "Put on makeup, glue on eyelashes, vomit, drive to work." She exhaled a stream of smoke. "Do you know how many men tell me I'm ugly? Me! Ugly!"

"They're mad," I said.

"Why are they mad?" she asked. "You tell me. Why are they mad?"

"For sport, I think."

She rapped her long pink nails on the table, a drumbeat of anxiety. "When my dancer permit runs out, I'm *not* renewing it."

"Krystal to the stage!" the DJ announced.

"Welp," she sighed, putting out her cigarette. And then, she leaned over, hugged me tight. Her body was sharp and hard and felt at once as if she could break at any moment or she could never break at all, bones of diamonds, flesh of gold.

Relax into the insanity—that's what the women in my family do.

Recently, I met with my cousin for dinner. I asked him what he remembered of my father's death. "Your mother was inconsolable," he said. "Arguably, she still is."

I've seen photos of us in the old days, before the hard times, the whole family at the beach, a cigarette between Mama's fingers, a smile on her lips. She was tanned and alive then. Young—younger than I am now. These days, Mama sits in a chair, orders baubles she can't afford from QVC and wears them nowhere. Relax into the insanity. It's what we do.

"The whole world opens up to you if you're beautiful," Mama told me, growing up. Mama was a pretty little girl, so pretty in fact that the local high school chose her to be its mascot. They even offered her a ride in the back of a convertible during a street parade. "I cried all day when I found out I'd been selected," Mama said; "I didn't know what a mascot was! But that night, Mama gave me the chicken breast at dinner, and she only took the wing."

Mama was alone—now and forevermore. When Daddy died, she bought a ticket to total surrender. Mama was just forty-three years old then. She'd never love again, so what was the point of living? She finally submitted to the extra pounds that had always troubled her whenever she was bold enough to stop starving—a crime for which I don't think she will ever atone. My childhood was dotted with refrigerator lights shining in the dark, illuminating women sneaking bites of food they didn't think they deserved in the light. "Growing up, Mama never ate," my mother has said of Granny Audrey. "I thought it was because we were poor. Now I see it won't poverty keeping food out of Mama's mouth."

My granny has always been beautiful, a crusade that will end only in death. When visiting her recently, I discovered a delivery of wrinkle cream on her doorstep. She was eighty-five at that time. On the far-flung occasions that I drag myself to Danville, the first thing she does upon seeing me is raise my shirt, congratulate me on staying thin. I'd like to say these accolades don't please me.

Relax into the insanity. Life is hard. That is our excuse, and it is our ticket. This ride is out of control. Let go. Accept. Melt. Let the tender insides of your heart take the shape of the wounds of the women who raised you.

Once, while student-teaching a class at University of Louisiana under the supervision of a senior professor, I taught a section from *The Sound and the Fury* that engages the theme of burgeoning female sexuality and the discord that emerges in its wake.

That awakening, that stepping into the body: a wedge shoved into any family. If a little girl is hard to love, even harder is a little woman.

As academics, we weren't supposed to reference the personal history that carved the shape of our scholarly interests. The personal was subjective, a story, not meant for display or analysis. Just ignore the fact that the guy in the wheelchair does disability studies and the single mother keeps crying over Hester Prynne. Yet nonetheless, in class that day, I could not resist. Out of my wet mouth issued the history of my body.

"Who else here was punished for being a slut?" I asked my fellow students. A few women tentatively raised their hands, glancing around the room.

Afterwards, the overseeing professor called me into her office. "That was inappropriate, don't you think?"

Too pretty to be good: my lot in life, my generational inheritance, an addiction to men translated as an addiction to beauty carved into the DNA. In my family, men don't stay. We fiend for them, terrified of their inevitable retreat. We clear the way for their leaving with our desperation for them to remain.

"You look just like him," my mama always told me of her father. I see her, age seven, counting the easy rhythm of his feet as he walked away. I see her, age seventeen, marrying her first husband Steve, her daddy giving her away as if she was his to give, one leaving man passing her off to another. I see her, age twenty-one, haggard and agonized as she sat by her daddy's deathbed, looking in his face for signs of love. "He loved me more than anybody," she has decided, and that is the verdict we carry. No man has been more treasured, more legendary, than this one, his greatness exaggerated by the distance he ran.

I read once that every woman was carried in the belly of her grandmother as an egg in the body of her mother. Likewise, her grandmother grew first in the womb of her great-great grandmother, our genes formed in the bodies of women that came hundreds of years before. The trials, the traumas, the pain, and the joy of the women who made me, stamped into my body: what my mama's mama learned to survive, so have I. It's in our blood, these secrets, these desires, these ways of moving through the world. We, daughters of our ancestors and mothers to generations to come, we carry the past, and within us, the past carves the future.

"What was he like?" I once asked Granny Audrey of her first husband, Mama's daddy, the man they could not keep.

"He wasn't a bad man," she answered. "He was just—too pretty to be good."

Once, the legend goes, Aunt Catherine ran smack dab into him in the Thalheimer's ladies' fashions section. He was looking for a dress in the wrong color, the wrong size. "That ain't for Audrey," Catherine whispered from over his shoulder. He jumped, caught off-guard elbow-deep in frills.

"If you don't tell her, I will," she warned.

He didn't, and she did.

Before my grandfather left one morning, the legend goes, Granny Audrey, then but a thin neat woman of thirty, snuck into the back of his sedan to ride along with him like a tick on a hound, silent and gorging. However, before she could shut the heavy door of the Chevy, my grandfather had already slid into the driver's seat.

At that time, remember, he was no grandfather, but instead a dark-eyed beauty with a crooked smile, a pressed shirt, and wavy black hair—Walter Shelton, the Elvis Presley of Danville, Virginia.

Afraid to alert him to her presence, Audrey didn't shut the door, didn't dare click that loud clack of the heavy metal. Instead, she rode on, crouched in the floorboard and holding onto the door in silence as Walter weaved his way through Evilland to the home of his mistress.

"No upper lip," Granny Audrey has said, of this woman. "She had no upper lip when she smiled."

With a honk of the horn, Walter summoned his lover. She sashayed from her front door right into the front seat. A goddamned blonde! What fury must Audrey have felt, watching this woman sidle up next to her husband, in the front seat of their car?

Yet even through this, she maintained her silence as onward they drove.

Perhaps it was the kiss that finally threw her over the edge. Perhaps it was the hungry way her husband's hands gripped that golden hair. Or maybe, maybe it was the way that blonde bitch sat regal in the front seat, as if she owned the car, the man, the life, the everything, as down Riverside Drive they drove.

Perhaps it was all of these reasons and more that incited the attack.

With a battle cry, Audrey leapt. With a shriek, she slung her purse above her head. With a holler, my granny rained blows upon the illicit couple, pocketbook landing with a sickening thud, again and again. The back door, no longer held by her hand, swung open; cars swerved.

Tires squealed—

Telephone pole—

Wood cracked—

Splinters rained—

Smoke streamed skyward from the crushed sedan, headlight glass sparkling upon the hot asphalt, as Audrey pulled herself from the gnarled vehicle, patted down her dress, and powdered her nose.

He'd be back that night, sorry as ever.

And then—he'd be gone again.

"Eventually, he stopped coming back at all," Mama finished.

"Well, you can't blame her for hating him," I said.

"Yeah," she replied, "but I can blame her for hating me."

Men. I couldn't keep them. Nor could I keep them away. I beckoned them to me, the black magic in my genes. "The Dodson hip-cock," my mama calls it, that way my aunts have of standing when a man walks by, hip popped, long leg stretched, eyes dreamy and smile bright. A careful concoction. There are layers to this legacy, but we don't have to learn them. We are born with them, instead.

Attracting men. Pushing them away. I fell in love with a man in the bayou. A good man with many commendable qualities, yet particularly attractive in his unavailability. Where I come from, sweetness is only sweetness when denied. Life feels like nothing without pain.

And yet, when after weeks and months of bewitchery, he at last became mine, and before us stretched only the future, no more bitter goodbyes, a silence befell my heart which I could not withstand. Hurt me, my beloved; gut me. If you do not rip me apart, this feels like nothing at all.

Wishes were granted, and he gutted me, after all. He delivered his blows softly, quietly, without malice, his head in his work, his eyes blind to me. Here was a man who once clutched me in the shadows and breathlessly confessed that he could not get enough of me. And now, as he took our baby from my arms and I headed to the strip club, it seemed he had had his fill. I'd carved my edges sharp. Turned into something he didn't want to explore. Become hard to hold.

I yearned to be wanted.

See me.

Not just the dairy cow I have become for our child.

Not just the body you fuck.

But also—

Look away.

He cooked me dinner each night, anyway.

And so, as my husband loved me quietly over a stove, I entertained other men. I chose not to inquire into any pain he might be hiding, and he returned in kind. Easier that way. Between us, a static grew, a white noise drowning the things we needed to say. I found ways to resent him; let me count the ways: he worked too late. He didn't call me pretty. He didn't ask how my night went. He went days, weeks without kissing me. I nursed these resentments, a sting to inject into our marriage, a pain to feel. In turn, he built his glass wall thicker. How many years would he deny me emotion, this man who had once loved me into madness in the heat of the deep south?

These resentments, hovering unsaid, covered like a blanket the precious memories of our early love. Covered the way, in the beginning, he couldn't get enough. Covered the way I couldn't have him, the thickest honey, the stickiest trap. Poem after poem pounded out in his name in the dark to the tune of a ticking clock counting the seconds of the days we had left together in the swamp. A hello that was a goodbye, a beginning that was always an end.

But we put an end to the end. We diverted the path. Unlike men are supposed to do, he did not leave.

And for this, I could not cease to punish him.

"You did well with that man," Krystal said, as I fanned out my earnings across the dressing room counter. "He wasn't interested in me."

"I can't imagine why not."

"You're more his type," she smiled. "You're smarter than everyone. Some men like that."

"And you're prettier than everyone. *All* men like that."

"Well, I earned it."

I looked to her face—lips swollen with injections, chest round with implants, stomach flat with starvation—and I nodded. Surely, she had earned it. I supposed she was an expensive woman to construct. In my heart this is a judgment against her, and an award for me: she is a cyborg; I am a human. She bought her beauty. I did not. The corner of my lash stabbed my eyeball and I peeled it off. "I suppose it is a lot of work to look as perfect as you," I answered, my diplomatic way of saying: you are a collection of doll parts.

"It wasn't as hard as you might think. All I had to do was sell my soul!"

"…three hundred, four hundred, five hundred," I counted under my breath.

"There was a boy I liked at church. He didn't like me back. Ever have one of those? A boy that didn't like you back?"

"Every single boy of my life."

"One day," she told me, "I chased him down. Cornered him in the sacristy. Said, hey boy, I got something to say to you. I couldn't have been more than nine, ten at the time.

He was older than me, rode a skateboard around the church parking lot after service. 'That boy is bad news,' my daddy said. So naturally, I wanted him. 'What do you want,' that boy asked me as I closed the door of the sacristy. Maybe it was the blue of his eyes, or the way he half-smiled; I don't know what it was that drove my bravery up—but I told him, 'You. I want you.'"

I stacked my money.

"And do you know what he did? He laughed right in my face—and told me I was ugly! And so, I decided that I was going to fix this problem. On the drive home from church that day, I told my daddy, 'I'm gonna pray to the Lord to make me pretty!'

"'God don't work that way,' Daddy answered.

"And so, I asked the Devil instead.

"It's hard to be an ugly little girl," she continued. "Sometimes, I think I've spent my whole life trying to fix that."

And that's how, one Sunday deep into the nineteen-eighties, Krystal locked herself in the bathroom, sat legs folded on the linoleum floor, leaned her forehead against the cool porcelain of the bathtub, and prayed to Satan.

"Dear Devil," she whispered, "if you make me beautiful, you can have my soul."

"And now," she concluded, "look at me!"

One could not argue—what God had refused, Lucifer had carved. Big in the right places, small in the others, lips parted, a body like glass. Smooth on the surface, sharp at the corners.

"Though I must say," she added, pulling from her locker a photo of her daughter, "my little girl looks just like I used to...."

"She's adorable," I replied.

Krystal blinked slow, shook her head. "Isn't she," she said.

"Dear Devil," Krystal had prayed, a lifetime ago on a bathroom floor, "if you make me beautiful, you can have my soul."

And everyone knows—the Devil always collect his debts.

My baby would cry when my husband arrived home. Eventually, he learned to weep in anticipation, tears starting the moment he heard his father's footsteps outside the door. It's not that they didn't share a bond. Dave sang lullabies for untold hours as I trudged across campus to teach another comp class or alternately stalked the club floor until the middle of the night. I often wondered if it were my absence that made me so precious.

I had become our son's world. At night, he slept with his fingers curled in my hair; in the morning, he woke to the rhythm of my heart, his mouth clamped on my breast, my life streaming into his own. When I'd return home from teaching, I'd rush to our bed to lay my hand on him, to make sure he hadn't disappeared. What fearful love had I injected into my heart by bringing this boy to life? Such affection filled me with preemptive agony. So much to be felt, such unguarded tenderness, all my love stacked like gold coins on the unstable scale of this child's life. Were he to fall, get sick, die—these things do happen—were that heart to stop beating, like a tower imploded from the foundation, all my coins would scatter. There was too much to lose.

And what must my son have thought, as each night I placed him into his father's arms and walked out the door? Babies have no sense of object permanence. They don't understand that what disappears often reappears. Did he lose me forever each night, and regain me anew each morning?

"Give me something to think about when I start to missing you," I used to tell my mama, when she'd get me ready for school.

"Rain drops on roses and whiskers on kittens," she'd sing. Those images never sufficed. In kindergarten, my teacher would lock me in the bathroom for disrupting class with my wailing grief. As I sobbed my way through the alphabet, my teacher slung me into the stall and turned the lock. I pounded the walls, hollering for Mama.

One Sunday, I expected Mama to stay home with me all day long, but she went to the grocery store instead. Daddy found me on the front stairs, mourning her absence with bitter tears. "Here," he said, handing me a dandelion he had picked from the concrete. "Look into this flower and see your mama's face."

I held onto that weed until it became a wilted tangle in my hand.

Never has there been a person more needed than Mama was by me, then.

As an ungenerous teenager filled with contempt, I looked back upon these years of childish adoration as a period she must have treasured—how delicious to be worshipped! Knowing her, she luxuriated in it!

Yet—perhaps I had been wrong? Perhaps I had consumed her, made a feast of her attention, hungrily devouring every inch of her as if she were mine. Perhaps she snuck to the grocery store to breathe, to think grown woman thoughts. Perhaps in her chest beat the same anxiety that now beat in mine as I gazed upon my sleeping son. Like me, perhaps she feared in her love for her child a goodbye that must await. Perhaps she kept her distance to protect us both. She warned me, when I became a mother, of the consequences of the bond I had created. "No one will break your heart like your child," she told me.

"You might find it mighty hard to leave that baby," Mama warned, when at six months postpartum I informed her that I was returning to teaching.

As I handed my son off to his father and headed into rush hour traffic to teach an evening class no one wanted to attend,

I smiled to my baby, planted a kiss on his cheek. "Give me something to think about when I start to missing you," I told him, and walked out the door.

My course at Tech had been added to the registration schedule late, my appointment to the position an afterthought. Consequently, my student body consisted almost entirely of last-minute registrations, students whose procrastination forced them to sign up for any old class remaining on the docket, regardless of their actual interest in the course topic. Freshman composition was a requirement, but this requirement was taught largely by post-doc fellows eager to prove their cutting-edge scholarship via obscure course themes that looked hip on job applications. My students had not enthusiastically signed up for "Unruly Women and the Politics of Representation." Instead, they had selected one of the few composition sections still available for registration.

In this way, the no-fucks-given procrastinators joined the last-minute hire in an unholy union.

Love was never meant for us. Love begins with choice.

Georgia Tech is an engineering school. These students—by and large—are not interested in poetry. These students, by and large, are also men.

On the second day of class, as I lectured upon gender politics, a student raised his hand and asked earnestly, "Wouldn't you say that the white man is the most oppressed person in America?"

That semester, the university became embroiled in a national scandal centering around an infamous "rape bait" email. In this email, a fraternity leader instructed his brothers on the art of luring intoxicated women into sex. These women he called "rape bait." News of this email hit nationwide. Outrage spread across the United States. Yet when I addressed this email with my class, almost unanimously they agreed—what a pity that these boys would lose their reputations over a joke.

Some people, they asserted, need to learn how to take a joke. Exhausted, I dismissed the class.

Clearly, I was among those lacking humor.

Relax into the insanity. Smile and act right. The students call me Lindsay. What an uppity bitch I must've seemed, demanding from them "doctor."

"There are no jobs for any of you," the department head told us, years ago. Yet, here we were. Yet here I stood, before twenty-eight young men, slinging lessons no self-respecting nineteen-year-old bro would give a fuck about, pandering for prestige, an attractive line in my CV. Here I stood, a doctor, yet before these young men, I felt like just another bitch.

Some people need to learn how to take a joke.

Relax into the insanity. Make the boys comfortable. Sacrifice my tender neck to the punchline in exchange for a paycheck, my payment for social ascendancy. I didn't get the professorship at Clayton State, Mama, but look—still I stand before the students of Georgia Tech, a school so fine that entire walls are made of whiteboard. Look at me. Look at how far I've come.

Look at how close I've stayed to home.

Nodding. Smiling. Rating my value low. Floating along the tide. Laughing at the joke. Make a nest out of your twisted pain and let it lull you to sleep. You'll wake in the morning just the same, and life will never have to change. Leave your baby at home. Leave your man behind glass. Transform into a painted lady on the weekends to feel like you're worth something. Kill yourself with poor decisions. Walk in silence along the groove carved out by the women who came before you. You'll never falter along this path. You'll always be good at this. This is who we are. This is who you have always been.

While taking a break from grading in my office at Tech one afternoon, I opened Facebook to discover that a man from the past had popped into my inbox—a guy I hadn't seen in half a lifetime. An old friend of Joey's, and thus, an old friend of mine. This friend was there when Joey beat me up, was present at the party when the night of terror began. He witnessed Joey sling me to the asphalt—saw him spit in my face—heard the rumors that Joey had been arrested— had accepted his phone calls from jail. "Maybe you shouldn't be so hard on him," this friend had suggested, then. I was seventeen.

Indignation filled my heart upon seeing his avatar in my inbox, and yet simultaneously I felt a strange fondness. Something ancient in me reasoned—well, he was caught in the middle. He was only twenty-two, maybe twenty-three, when it happened—maybe too young to understand right from wrong? Indeed, one could say that I had been a drama queen, was continuing to reign drama even now, in my current anger. They called me that back then, you know: a drama queen.

After all, Joey never hit me in the face.

I never felt that I received the full ass-beating I had coming.

I am not so pure as the world demands.

Is that why my heart pounded, to see this ghost from the past in my inbox, this friend from an evil era?

Perhaps he came with only a casual hello?

I opened the message, and I found instead:

"This is Joey. Rodney let me use his account to send you this. I knew you wouldn't open the inbox if you saw it was from me."

He congratulated me on my apparent success: the doctorate, the husband, the child. "I want you to know," he continued, "that all that stuff between us—that's in the past now."

That stuff between us—

Is in the past now?

My God. He's here to absolve me.

Perhaps I should be the bigger person. Perhaps I should write him a kind word back. I was a grown woman. Perhaps I needed to relax. Needed to leave the past where it belonged, like normal people do. There is still that pull to please him, after all these years, to give him the comfort he seeks.

No.

I see myself, sixteen, getting railed by Joey in the back of Daddy's car; Daddy's body won't even cold yet. Joey was twenty then. "My dad's dead too," he said, a seduction. I see me, barely seventeen, Joey's hand around my throat in the pouring rain. "I have to hide these bruises," I wrote in my diary, "or else Mama will really be mad!" I see me, seventeen, Joey's spit smeared across my face, a crack like lightning splitting the night in half, my friend's fist sending him spinning beneath the glow of a single street lamp. I see me, a child, crouched in the back bedroom of Joey's mama's house as he pummeled my ribs and I prayed for salvation from a God to whom I'd long felt loathsome and profane. A child then, hiding in a basement to meet my abuser days before his sentencing in order to fuck him once more. He kept his shoes on when he fucked me that afternoon. He kept his pants on, too, strapped around his thighs. Me, however, he stripped buck-naked as he pinned me down, fucking my battered body with a roar.

A rage rose into my chest, a fire.

That stuff's in the past?

Never.

I slammed my laptop shut.

The following class, I arrived late to find a surprise.
Across the whiteboard it spread, proud and jeering:
A ten-foot-long, veiny, hairy-balled, ejaculating dick.
Around me, my students chuckled under their breath.
For a moment, I stood silent, shocked.

What has happened here, I wondered, dazed. Had my own students drawn…? No. This doesn't happen to actual doctors. This doesn't happen to women who act right. This—wasn't happening. My mind reeled through my options. I must, of course, take the proper course of action.…

Should I laugh, act like one of the gang? Should I ignore it entirely, a false attitude of detachment? What behavior was the proper course of action for a lowly post-doc who needed good student evaluations in order to continue in her field?

I felt the students' eyes upon me. These boys who called me "Lindsay." These kids in boat shoes and button-ups. The ilk of Forest Hills, all grown up, the world so clearly theirs for the taking that not one gave a second thought to drawing a ten-foot dick across a classroom to confront the only female in attendance, also their professor.

Recently, on another unpleasant holiday visit to Danville, I encountered the former mayor's son in the local bar, a boy who'd ridden my school bus and taunted me relentlessly. Laughing, he asked me if I remembered the time I "did that crazy thing." I asked him what he was referring to, and he answered, howling, "You attacked me with period blood!" Around him stood four other men, who erupted into disgusted groans. I lied and told him no, I did not remember any such thing. However—I *did* remember. I committed that assault; sure I did. He had laughed at me one too many times, and so I reached my hand down my pants, collected what was flowing, and attacked him with my blood. I failed to land my aim entirely accurately. Some of the blood ended up swiped on the seat. That stain remained on the bus for weeks. Months. Years. Forever.

And now, these students, in their boat shoes and button-ups, were having a chuckle over *me*? Coming at *me* with a dick?

"I don't think you people know who the fuck I am," I announced.

They fell silent.

Eyes shifted.

Even here, in the hallowed halls of the academy, the place I thought would be my escape from the sordid history of my body—a bad body, a female body, a body that invited insulting dicks—even here, I receive this disrespect? If I had not this female body, would there be a dick on my wall? I came to write poetry. I came to make art. I came not to service rich boys. I came not to grade plagiarized essays.

Telling disbelieving men about my dissertation while topless. Getting choked by a fetishist in a closet; getting paid *and* fired for it. Wearing a suit to teach a class of men in an impotent effort to make them see me as a doctor and not just some fucking broad. Just some broad, wherever I went, no matter what degree I obtained. Indeed, sometimes I thought the degrees made it worse, made the men even madder. Relax into the insanity. Laugh along with the boys. Be one of the gang. Make it easy. Demand nothing. Student evaluations matter when securing a non-temporary position. Well guess what. I don't want a non-temporary position. I don't even want *this* position.

"F's all around," I declared, as with one long swipe of the eraser in, I cut the dick in half and walked out the door.

I quit this bitch.

CHAPTER TWELVE
THE PURGE

I got hit by a car when I was a child. The accident happened over the holidays of my eighth year.

Mama had a taste for nice things. For Christmas, she gave me a sapphire ring. I hardly knew what to do with such a precious gem, but I could tell by the light in her eyes that I should treasure it.

At that charge, I failed.

Two days later, as my cousin Meredith and I excavated potato bugs from the dirt, I made a terrible discovery:

Upon my ring finger, the setting for the sapphire languished, hideous and blank.

The jewel—was lost.

"Mama's going to kill me," I said, and raced across the park.

At home, trouble surely awaited. I have never been one to put off the pain. Instead, I barrel towards it.

The last thing I remember before the world went black: Meredith's scream, a *no* shouted into a blue sky.

Tires squealed; a child flew; a single shoe spun across the sky—or so I have been told. I myself did not attend the impact. The force of blow turned my mind dark. Even the gravest injury can occur without pain if delivered with striking, blinding ferocity.

"That car had to be going forty miles an hour," a witness would later say.

When I awoke, I found myself strapped to a board. Above me stood Daddy, fondling a single white Ked.

"You should've seen him," Meredith would say, later. "He jumped clear over the cactus patch to get to you. He won't hardly wearing any clothes at all."

Daddy must have been cold that day, a scant two days after Christmas, standing in the street in only shorts and no shirt.

When I returned home from the hospital, I reported immediately to my diary.

"Today, I was hit by a car. It was the worst thing to ever happen to me."

My head ached from the concussion; my forehead burned with road rash—nonetheless, I grinned, electrified, inspired, daydreaming. Oh, what a tale I would spin for my classmates upon our return from Christmas break! Perhaps they'd visited grandmas, received robots for gifts; perhaps some had even obtained the coveted Barbie Dream Mansion. However, I alone possessed this showstopper of a tale. I'd barely felt the hit. The bruises would fade. Yet the story—would remain. Stories gave the moment meaning, turned a vast chaos into a parable, a justification for pain, an outlet for pleasure. When the teacher would ask us, inevitably, of our activities over the holiday, I would answer with grave seriousness, to the immeasurable admiration of my peers:

"I—got hit by a car."

I fled the academy with the stunning unprofessionalism reserved for those who no longer give a fuck. When my superiors at Georgia Tech requested an exit interview, signatures, the proper protocol for quitting, I ignored them. Such abnegation of responsibility would ensure that no academic institution would ever hire me again. I wanted it that way.

I didn't know what exactly I would do with my life.

But—I had secret desires.

"This is my chance," I admitted to Dave, finally.

"Your chance for what?"

"To do something with my life. To become someone. To write."

"You won't apply for another academic position?"

"No. I will continue to strip in the meantime."

"In what meantime?"

"In the meantime between now and whenever I remember who the fuck I am."

As always, he trusted me in this endeavor.

But as each shift began, my body revolted, shook, grew ill.

I ate benzos to chill.

Stripping—used to be easier than this. When I was a kid, a teen, a twenty-something wild thing—stripping was easier than this. But now, post-thirty, post-academy, years deep into my second season of stripper life—

My heart pounded the moment I hit the floor. Perhaps my anxiety had increased with age. Certainly, my indignation. Maybe staying up all night didn't have the same appeal. I couldn't pinpoint what, exactly, caused this shift of feeling, this move from party-time to hellhole. There were examples:

Indulging some nice guy's violence in exchange for a higher placement on a tip-out sheet. Pathetic. I wanted out. A drunken bachelor, cross-eyed, puked into his cocktail glass as I undulated inches from his face. Degrading. I wanted out. A bored rich kid, almost certainly a Chad, or perhaps a Brad, denied me his eyes while I danced for him, a deliberate humiliation. I wanted out.

Yet my desire to retire was rivaled only by my fear of leaving a woman I loved behind. I hadn't always *needed* to be in the club, not financially—but I had always needed the club in *me*. Who would I be, if not Lux? She'd saved me, hardened me, stood by my side. Tall. Powerful. An idol carved in stone. An Amazon stalking the earth. I knew her. I invented her. Where was she now? What had once been so easy—going to these men's tables, sitting down, inviting myself into their night, a fine and complex art—now stretched out before me like a deadly expanse of wilderness dotted through with wolves.

I can't talk to these motherfuckers tonight.

Yet—

I must.

I would not die behind a desk, a fool holding tight to a dream that was never her own. "There's no telling what you could create, *will* create," Dr. Moore had told me, a promise that dogged me still. Mama had talent, too; did she ever tell you? Mama writes country music songs. I had my daddy's blood in me, too. The drive to fix engines. The energy to create. I, too, scribbled art into the night. I, too, refused to disappear.

"Don't forget me," I would plead into the darkness of my bedroom, an insomniac child whispering prayers to the future, halfway through puberty and already one foot in the grave. I searched the mirror those long fearful nights, finding in my reflection a friend. She speaks to me even now, from a different life, in a different town, a place I couldn't sleep then and I can't sleep now. Her. It is to her I am bound.

"I will strip to pay the bills," I told my husband, as I pounded into the keyboard these very pages.

Unlike me, Dave hadn't bothered with a PhD. For three years, he'd worked as a gopher at an accounting firm, fetching coffees for bosses while counting rejections from high school teaching positions, a soul-crushing endeavor. However, weeks before our son's birth, a job offer came. Dave did not care for the prestige of a doctorate. He did, however, desire something greater than fetching coffee for CPAs. So when a private religious school offered him a position, despite his rampant atheism, he accepted.

At Dave's new school, girls and boys were not allowed to touch. A woman like me would not fit in at any of his professional functions, I imagined. On the one occasion I attended an event, I accidentally shook the hand of the holiest man in attendance— forbidden, taboo, for me to pollute a holy man with my female hand. He accepted my slight graciously, but I burned with embarrassment. My god, what if this holy man knew the extent of my crimes? He'd be hand-washing all day!

Around this time, at the grocery store, I found a Mother's Day card. It read, "Thanks mom, I'm not in prison and I'm not a stripper!"

In a burst of rebellious self-love, I placed on my car a bumper sticker of a woman on a pole. I drove around town chin high, daring anyone to stare, wanting them to stare. *Yes. I am the whore you hate.*

Yet, when Dave borrowed my car, he taped a school emblem over the stripper sticker.

For months, I accepted this in silence.

I knew what the world thought of me.

However, one day—I got mad.

Maybe I thought he ought to parade me around somewhere. Maybe I thought his love was too quiet. Whatever it was, I told him at last:

"That offends me, when you cover up my sticker."

"You need to understand the world I'm operating in," he pleaded.

"Understood," I said, and then silently carried that resentment for years.

One day, he came home from work, stricken. "There's a problem," he said.

"We have become aware of your wife," an anonymous parent from his school had emailed. "This is not the kind of problem we expected to deal with at a school of this caliber."

Not again. Please Jesus, don't let me be a problem again. And yet—it is too late. And yet—I already am.

"I'm sorry," I sputtered, horrified, sickened—

And then, I stewed all night.

What apology would he give for me, his whore wife? Would he lose his job? And if he did—if I had gone so terribly far as to cause my husband and father of my child to lose his job—would he then…divorce me? Leave me?

I felt miserably sorry, on the one hand.

On the other hand, I seethed with rage.

I ran away from the academy because I refused to obey the rules and regulations of a proper society to which I'd never belonged. And now some "concerned parent" I'd never met sought to control my behavior via a job that wasn't even mine? This school didn't pay me. I'd signed no moral contracts. My husband had just been voted Teacher of the Year. How dare anyone judge his wife? How dare anyone judge me?

I directed my anger not only at the school, but at my husband, as well. He had, after all, covered up my sticker. Thus, I reasoned, he implicitly agreed that I was a problem. As he sat silent across the room, walled in glass, I imagined that at that very moment he concocted ways to explain away my awfulness, explanations by which he could distance himself from me. Perhaps he'd take our wedding photo down from his desk. Stop telling the kids he had a wife. "I'll ask her to be more discreet," I imagined him saying, and then sitting me down for a good solid talking-to about what's appropriate.

He didn't sleep that night, and neither did I.

When he arrived home the next day, the greyness in his face was replaced with a healthful pink. He hummed as he set his lunchbox down, loosened his tie.

"Well?" I asked.

"Well what?"

"Did you get called into the office?"

"No. I went to the office on my own volition."

"You told them about the email?"

"I did."

"And did you apologize?"

"Apologize?" he asked. "You're my wife. You are not something to apologize for."

"This is my first time getting one of these," said the handsome man when I offered him a dance. "I'm not sure what to do."

"*I* know what to do," I replied, "and that's all that matters."

He surveyed my body with admiration as I moved before him, his eyes travelling across hills and valleys until finally they met mine.

"I hope this isn't offensive," he began, and I steeled myself for the blow, "but your belly…and your breasts…the stretch marks.… I can tell you're a mother—and it's just—very beautiful to me." Is this kindness, your words? Is this tenderness, your admiration of my imperfections? Is this love, or something like love? As I surveyed my own body in the mirror, I couldn't help but agree. I am beautiful. I was born beautiful. I will die beautiful.

I had sought in every man's glance a recrimination. I expected ultimately their revulsion. Had other kindnesses existed which I had not seen?

Why did I think my husband didn't want me? He was looking for something different when he came to the swamp. In that depth of mud and earth, in that place of viscous protoplasm where pools of water grew skins and vines hung leaves as big as bodies, he found me. There had only been one woman before me. He had never smoked a cigarette, never done a drug, never disappointed his parents. He came from a place where winters were cold and so were emotions. His people were polite, kind, but closed off. Once I told his mother she was beautiful, and she looked as if she'd been slapped in the face. People don't talk that way up there. People up North are different, Mama always said; they don't love like we do.

They don't love like we do, an ocean crashing, consuming, pulling you spinning beneath the surface, tossing you every which-a-way but loose. They don't love like we do, heavy and wet, scary and suffocating, an infinite depth of crushing darkness. Where I come from, we learn early on how to occupy the void. We know death. We are the evidence of goodbye. We are what remains.

They don't love like we do. Instead, they cook dinner. Instead, they don't pry. They step back, stoic, and let your storms pass. They don't run. A Midwesterner loves a good squall. They know that underneath the clouds resides still the sky. They know that *you* are the sky.

He didn't want me, I told myself; he'd signed up for a better woman I'd promised to deliver. *My husband expected an English professor when he married me*, I joke to all who will listen. "If I don't get into a PhD program," I'd told him, years ago, "I won't know who I am."

"You'll remember pretty quickly," he'd said.

Here was me. All of me. Yes, even this. Yes, even this woman naked in a closet. I had tried to erase her. Escape her. Deny her. Felt guilty for loving her. Called my love for her pathetic. Dined upon my beauty in the mirror, only to purge later. How dare I still be a slut, I'd scolded myself. How could I desire even still the eyes of these men? Why—why—*why* could I not fix myself? I'd gotten the fucking degrees. I'd married a good man. I'd had a baby. All the right steps, I'd taken. And yet— here she was. Again. Naked before a man whom she will never see again. And yet here she was, that woman in the mirror, an apparition I'd created as both a treasure and a weapon. I'd named her both god and destroyer. Perhaps, she was both.

"You really are something," the handsome man whispered, wonder in his voice like a man gazing at the night sky.

The night sky is required reading for any man who seeks to know me.

"Wow. Who else can say they've seen their English professor naked?"

At the tip rail, a young woman laid down two twenties.

"Freshman Comp, Georgia State," she said. "You were the coolest teacher ever."

When teaching in the university, I would sometimes find among my students a young woman nodding silently in the back of class. Telling me, in the simplest of ways: I feel you; I'm listening. There were enough years between us, enough lived experience, to inhibit us from being peers, these young women and me. I never felt at liberty to properly thank them, afraid to breach some professional boundary. Yet, here, in this club, those restrictions fell away. I was no longer the teacher. She was no longer the student. Here, we were just two women, one grown and one not quite.

"Why'd you quit teaching?" she asked, when I dismounted the stage and joined her at her table.

"If I had a room full of students like you, I might have stayed."

"I always admired you," she said, looking to her lap, afraid to meet my eyes. "And now... I'd like to work with you."

"I'm of two minds when it comes to initiating the innocent."

"Dr. Byron," she said, "I am not innocent."

I too was once a feral child filled with the blood of the ancestors, sacred whores materializing in my artwork like cave drawings, imprinting ancient intelligence upon a child's scrawl. Had I forgotten what it was like, to feel this pull?

Tits out at eight a.m. for English class: the kid wasn't innocent. The boys in the class always gathered 'round. Like me, she was born for this. Bred for this. Rewarded for her face. Rewarded for her body. Attention granted most enthusiastically when playing sex clown. Billboards showcasing rib bones had her denying herself early on the things she didn't deserve—deliciousness, not allowed. Fuck cupcakes. Real women survive on air. Our labor is laughing at jokes that aren't funny. We are the supporting beams of the machine, keeping the old dudes smiling. A thousand dollars? That might as well be a million to her, but it's a penny to these old dudes. They can afford it. She can earn it. Not every woman can; not every woman will. Not every woman will practice the dark arts. No, the kid is not innocent.

"How do I get on your level?" she asked.

Vanity tempted me to feign humility, giggle *oh whatever do you mean*, request implicitly a list of compliments I'd quite enjoy to hear. But I know already the fabric of her admiration. She doesn't have to tell me; I remember. The mane of hair. The long stride. Twirling in these shoes. A confidence that announces, *I know how shit works*. I figured out the game. I cracked the code. I have embodied feminine perfection via stunning artifice, and the fools in the audience believe illusion to be truth. I know what she sees, this twenty-something child, and my heart fills and breaks at once to envision the image she holds of me. I, too, stood once where she now stands, gazing upon a god of my own making, a human being as warped and hurt as any of us, a real person upon whom I airbrushed the image of a fantasy.

How do you get on my level?

First, my girl, you must fit a certain mold—but don't worry, you've got that. You're a pretty girl. You've always been a pretty girl. You're not too fat and you're not too thin and you're not too sad and you're not too happy; you're a fantasy dressed up in potentiality: you can be whatever they want you to be. Be like water, Bruce Lee said: water becomes whatever you pour it into. Water can flow and water can crash. Water changes landscapes, shapes the earth—steady, slowly, but forever. Be like water—become whatever vessel he desires. You have carved a river over everything you've touched.

I took her wine from her hand, finished it with one great swallow. Into the empty flute, I poured my leftover beer, golden and foamy in the long-stemmed glass.

"Look," I said. "Now it's champagne."

She parted her lips to speak, embarrassed, longing to confess. Spend enough years in this life and you discern quickly the look of love. "You—are—*goals*," she told me at last, with the grave seriousness of a millennial. I laughed as if this compliment didn't faze me. It did.

I am a woman with a past. Yet in me, the kid sees greatness. Soon, my young friend, I will remove these lashes, this hair, this mask, and the god you see before you will disintegrate into dust. In her place will remain a person made of blood and secrets.

There are hours to go before I sleep.

As I watched her survey the floor with wonder, with the anticipation of a dreamer on the edge of possibility, I felt tempted to chalk up her attraction to naivety; she's a kid who doesn't know any better. But the truth is—I get it. The glamour she witnesses is real. When dollars fly, and the crowd loves you—of course it feels good. One could argue that beneath this pleasure works always the machine. Men own this club, after all. We pay them for the privilege of pleasing their customers. My thrill on this stage, this thrall of ecstasy: all rewards for playing correctly my role in the game. Of course they throw dollars when you stay thin and sling hair. Women's attention for sale—but only the pretty ones, the young ones, the ones ripe for ruin. Yes. My role is clear. Both god and destroyer, yes. I have known this always. I have known this all along.

"You talk to that lady to audition," I told my young friend, as Kelly strolled by, clipboard in hand.

"I'm scared. What do I do?"

"Not much. Get naked in a closet for that lady in the suit. If she thinks you're good enough, then you dance on stage, and then a manager judges you. If he thinks you're good enough, then—"

"But—I don't have anything to wear—"

"Don't worry," I told her; "I've got you."

"You won't be seeing me here much longer," I told Krystal as we changed into our street clothes. She nodded, just as exhausted as me.

I shoved my stripper shoes into my bag and sank against the make-up counter.

"I just—," I began, then put my head in my hands. "I just—I just do this because—"

Do you understand me, Krystal? Does your brain scramble and your hips ache? Do you find yourself forever drawn to this place, regardless? Is this place all you have ever known? My sister. Do you understand me? Is this place all you have ever known?

"I just do this because—I just—do this because—"

"Lux," she said, placing gently her finger to my lips, "I know why you do this."

We start off claiming "I won't do this forever," and we wake up, decades later, a lifetime and an instant all at once, and realize—*we have*. We *have* done this forever. The months we used to count from our initiation we now count to our retirement. We pull our ponytails tight to smooth out the wrinkles on our forehead and squeeze out every last shift we can from this dwindling goldmine, our lifelong career, this place in the world that becomes our place in the world when we forsake normal life for hoe life.

It felt like yesterday, getting jerked up at the Styxx, the housemom's nails digging into my arm. *Didn't they teach you anything?* Like yesterday, watching my crumpled car disappear into the darkness as I counted cash in the back of a taxi and thought I was rich. Like yesterday, taking an hour to apply false lashes, weeping from frustration and poked eyeballs throughout. Raw material: all ambition, strange vanity, and charisma, no wisdom to temper this sword.

Sometimes you don't know that you're learning until it's all said and done. Until you can view the thing solid, whole, like a painting on a wall. See how far you've come. You've spent your life trudging, head down. Finally, you look up, and notice the world has changed. In the mirror, you discover—the world is not the only thing that's changed.

I'd spent my life employing sex as power. On some fronts I'd succeeded—acquisition of money, of course, but more than that, a feeling of control. No one can hold me. I will make my own way. Anger churned always beneath the surface. I took pride in my pain. I placed my hardships like play-pretties on a shelf, a display for visitors, a depository of toys for when I was bored. Daddy called me a whore one day in nineteen ninety-four, but he also wrote "Lindsay" all over his workroom in painstaking calligraphy: which name had I chosen to count? What level of perfection had I expected from him? What level of perfection had I expected from any of them—Mama, Granny Audrey, Bill, my husband—the women who raised me, the men who loved me? I blamed my family for their flaws, blamed my men for their own, yet here I was, a grown woman forever outrunning the hurricane I'd been at thirteen.

Lord knows I'd tried to fix myself.

Tried to correct my whoredom with prestigious jobs and terminal degrees.

Yet the enigma in Blue Cyan beckoned evermore.

She would not disappear should I refuse to acknowledge her.

A woman on a pedestal will not go unseen.

Hello, my god, my torturer. I cannot extinguish your light. I thought loving you wasn't allowed. I hid the pictures I drew by the moon. In secret I have loved you, this whole life. I cannot justify as righteous the things I have done. I do not wish to try, not for one moment longer, to justify as righteous anything at all.

Before me, hours stretched before dawn. Once home, I would sit in the waning darkness and write, as I have done, these many years, the clock ticking the rhythm of everyone else's sleep but my own. I would write of Krystal's finger upon my lips, a poem. I would write of a handsome man who called me beautiful. I would write of a former student wearing my sequin bikini; I would write of Krystal praying on the bathroom floor. Krystal had dealt with the Devil. I'd dealt with the Devil, too. He'd given me pain, and he'd given me a song. I paid for creation in the coin of agony. Artists are supposed to hurt. That is what Daddy had always been trying to tell me—in his life, in his death. I didn't know how much longer I could continue on like this. My body ached; my mind suffered. This was a job for a younger woman. A woman I used to be. A woman who existed still and forevermore on a timeless plane. She would drive me ever forward, night after night, as long as I needed her to. *Write*, she told me, my friend in the mirror, *write all of this down when you get home.*

When at long last our lives become predictable, a comfortable nest of family and home, the mind has a way of harkening back to wild days, hard days, days on fire, when nothing was certain and everything screamed.

Much of the time I wrote, I wrote about Bill. I suppose we do this, the aging, the married, the women promised against lives they will never again have; I suppose occasionally we reminisce in solitude on the fires we have forsworn.

"What are you up to," my husband asked, finding me at the kitchen table at dawn, narrating the passion of the early two-thousands into Microsoft Word.

"Oh, just writing."

Sometimes, gluttoned on nostalgia, horrified to be old, I'd flee the manuscript to hide weeping in the bathroom. We, who had once been children howling into the night, reduced now only to representations in the form of letters and lines? Was that all any of us could ever wish for? To be a character in someone else's story? I imagined what I would say to Bill were I ever to see him again. I wouldn't, I imagined, ever see him again. It is possible we will die without ever seeing each other again. I wondered if he'd ever looked me up. I wondered if he'd ever thought about messaging me.

He had.

My heart leapt to find him one morning, hidden in the spam folder of my inbox.

"Hello, stranger," he wrote.

He'd never been married, he told me.

And he'd never forgotten me, either.

At the end of the note, he left his phone number.

I had not seen him since that night at the pizza joint, a final moment I didn't know was final. A different world then, a different existence. I was a girl covered in spikes, hurt and furious. He was a boy, thin and tall and scared to death of me.

I sat on his message for a week, not knowing what to do.

And then, I remembered.

Nine days on a couch, balls of white bread stuffed into my mouth. I remembered: my handprint on his face. His smile, that one crooked tooth, the circular tattoo between his shoulder blades. I'd been hated, and ruined, and orphaned, and beaten, and he came into my life with softness, with sweetness. I could not then accept softness, sweetness. I was too young, too hurt, too goddamned feral, to love right.

I contemplated my response for many days.

But I had always known what I would say.

"For years, I have promised myself that I would tell you what you've meant to me if I ever had the chance," I wrote him at last, "and this looks a lot like the chance."

And then I told him:

I have photos of us. I keep them in a trunk. I look at them still. I take them out only when alone. My god, were you ever beautiful. You were the most beautiful man, and everyone knew it but you. There has never been a day since I met you that I have not loved you. Can you believe that we are now old? Can you believe that once we were young?

That's the thing about it, young love. It teaches you. It touches you. It leaves a mark. This is what love can feel like, you learn at nineteen, wild and naked in your first apartment, nobody to stop you from melding with this man. This man, who touches me soft. This man, who cries when I speak sharp. This man, who will take punishment from me until he can't take anymore. But before he can't take anymore: there is a box fan. A bowl of ice. Sweaty sheets. A joint on his lip. Love all day. Photos to fondle in solitude for the rest of your life.

And also, I told him:

I'm married now, and we have a son.

His response was prompt. "I'm not going to impede your greatness or complicate your peace," he wrote. "You were, after all, always destined for greatness."

"Seize your happiness, Lindsay Erin Burton," he signed off, by way of goodbye. "You have always deserved it."

For years, I have wondered, does he love me with the depth I love him, all these years away from love on the floor?

The answer is yes.

He loves me, even still.

He loves me as he walks away.

"You are the second coming of Bill," I joke with my husband, from time to time. He tolerates my teasing with more generosity than anyone could expect. I don't mean to suggest him a replacement, a stand-in, an *I-guess-you'll-do* for a man who came before. After all, the man who came before exists for me now as an artifact in my heart, frozen forever at twenty-two. Longing has a way of coloring our memory, turning humans into art. Here, in this bed, however, sleeps a person. He does not shine with the well-tended luster of a museum display. He breathes, and twitches, and kicks off the blankets, every night the Lord sends. Many men have laid by my side and left as quick as they arrived. Rare and precious, those who have loved me with real love, not just body love; precious, those who made me feel chosen and not an aberration, not a horror to flee. "I can't wait another minute to see you," Bill grinned, skipping work to make love to me on the floor. "I can't get enough of you," Dave whispered into my neck one hot night in the bayou. You are the second coming of love, my husband, our hands clasped together, a goodbye written on the other side of hello, a promise to stay that no mortal can ever make. I bring the clouds, and you—you commit to the sky.

Seize your happiness, Lindsay Erin Burton.

You have always deserved it.

I wasn't there when Daddy died. Like many memories, my recollection of this is a story, a scene I've spun based on my mama's telling, a scene that stalks my heart like a shadow, a movie of my own invention. Who can know how many tubes ran through his body at the end? Who will tell how thin he became? Who could comprehend my daddy small and weak? When death was finished with him, I refused even to look upon his corpse. At my request, the funeral was closed casket. Mama told me he made art right until the very end, sketching the birds that flitted outside his window. I wouldn't know. I wasn't there.

I see him now, my daddy, a baby squirrel in hand, one rough thumb stroking his fur, head bent in tender affection. My daddy, saving a puppy from the storm. "It's the shadows on things that make them beautiful," he told me once, looking upon one of my drawings. With his leaving, a shadow stretched across my life and never lifted. I would be an artist all of my days.

By the time Daddy died, he had been unconscious nearly a week. "He will never wake," the doctors advised Mama; "you know what you must do." And so, she crawled into the hospital bed with him, snuggled next to his side as he slept, as she had been denied in life. She knew what this was. This was goodbye.

And yet, he would not die.

The machines were shut off, and yet—

He would not die.

Daddy wasn't a dying man. He wasn't the leaving kind.

"You have to tell him it's okay for him to go," the nurse told Mama.

"But it's not okay for him to go!"

"Well, he needs it to be."

And so, Mama snuggled closer. Stroked his face. Told him, David, we will be okay. I will be okay. Lindsay will be okay. And though he had been asleep for days, at these promises, tears streamed from his eyes. So, he could hear, after all. So, he was in there, after all.

And then, he wasn't.

It's an amazing thing about dying. How there are two people in a bed, and then, there is one.

Life—disappears.

Why did I marry this man with your name, Daddy, when I could lose him? Why did I have this child with your eyes, Daddy, when I could lose him? They will both leave, in one way or another. You taught me that.

Don't love anyone. Close every door.

Or—

Open every door.

Create because death. Kiss because death. Tickle baby because death. Make love because death. Hold me. Let's go on vacation. One of us will die; there is no time to waste. Every adventure, the sound of a ticking clock as its soundtrack, the memory of your quick departure, my starting point.

You disappeared. I know you didn't want to go. I'm sorry I never told you goodbye. I didn't know that the last time I saw you would be the last. You held my hand and I remember your skin, the bigness of your palm, the strength of your grasp. I was scared to tell you then how much I loved you.

You taught me to ride the waves when I was little. You told me to drive above the speed limit. You encouraged me to ride my bike fast down the hill. I fell off that bike doing that. Mama grew up afraid, swaddled in life jackets at the edge of the tide; you grew up hard, scared of nothing. Every risk, this path I've carved out of the wilderness: the fruit of your blood in my veins.

There's a photo of you on my wall—in it, you're young, younger than I ever knew you. You lean out a window, mischievous, a crooked grin on your face, turquoise rings on your fingers. I tell my son: that's *my* daddy. That's the man who taught me to cuss. That's the man that saved animals. That's the man who could fix any lawnmower. He was fun. He was adventure. He was unruly. Let's run until our lungs burn, son, one part my daddy and one part my husband—two men who share the same name, two men who created the same boy, two men who loved me, one who loves me still.

You could speak to the birds, too, Daddy, hold entire conversations with the forest.

You—were one of the wild things.

And guess what?

So am I.

Note from the author

I lived this story. It is my honor to tell it.

This is a work of creative nonfiction. I have written with the priority of creating a work of art rather than a work of journalism. Some names of places and people are changed, and some minor characters are composite.

I find myself afraid to publish this work, and that fear has kept me sitting on this manuscript for years. What might people think? Who will be mad at me? How dare I write about these people? To my husband, my son, my mother, my grandmother, my brothers, my aunts, my cousins, my ancestors, my fellow dancers, and particularly my dead father, who plays a starring role in this story, as dead fathers are wont to do: you influenced my life so thoroughly that I could not tell a story of myself without you in it. Thank you.

November 2020
Lindsay Byron
aka Lux ATL